Popular Mechanics

HOW TO CHARM A BIRD

**Popular
Mechanics**

HOW TO
CHARM A BIRD

CREATE A BACKYARD HAVEN
with BIRDHOUSES, BATHS,
& FEEDERS

BY THE EDITORS OF POPULAR MECHANICS

HEARST BOOKS
A division of Sterling Publishing Co., Inc.

New York / London
www.sterlingpublishing.com

CONTENTS

Foreword 7

Introduction 9

CHAPTER 1
SPRING AND SUMMER 13

CHAPTER 2
FALL AND WINTER 41

CHAPTER 3
GOOD EATING 63

CHAPTER 4
HOME SWEET HOME 97

CHAPTER 5
BATHING BEAUTIES 129

CHAPTER 6
PROTECTING FEATHERED FRIENDS 145

CHAPTER 7
SPOTTING BIRDS 159

Index 168

FOREWORD

I f you've ever spent a relaxing hour or two just sitting on a porch watching the busy movements of the birds that make your yard their home, you've experienced the singular fascination of birding. And if, like so many other people, you find joy in observing these wonderful creatures, you might want to attract more birds into your yard and to keep them there as long as possible.

Like any visitors, birds of all types are drawn in by the offer of a place to clean up after a day's labor, a good meal, and safe, hospitable lodging. But convincing birds to live in your backyard oasis is harder than it seems. *How to Charm a Bird* reveals the practical tips and little-known tricks necessary to lure birds of every feather into your yard and garden.

The information and projects compiled here have been mined from the *Popular Mechanics'* archives. Even though some of our advice dates back almost a hundred years, birds haven't changed a whole lot over that time. A wren or purple martin still wants the same type of birdhouse in which to nest, their diets have remained the same, and they still need the same protection from predators such as cats.

But we think the stylized period illustrations and interesting asides add something special to the topic. In our busy, turbo-charged lives, this little book reminds us that there is a real benefit to taking some time to slow down and notice what's going on in our own backyards, and in some cases, even to become beneficial companions to our winged guests.

The Editors of *Popular Mechanics*

INTRODUCTION

B irding is the hidden gem among nature-focused pastimes. Although it doesn't get much press, the leisurely pursuit of observing these frenetic, amusing, antic and ultimately quick-moving creatures is the perfect way to "get back to nature." It is an exercise that both calms the soul and heightens the senses—it forces you to become quieter and more observant (two abilities that are often grossly underestimated in this harried modern world). In the process, you get the chance to relax and learn how fascinating birds can be.

And they are fascinating. Birds are simply some of the most engaging and amusing members of the animal world. Between the dramatic majesty of an eagle swooping down to grab a fish from the surface of a lake and the incredibly soothing background sound of a songbird calling for a mate there lies an amazing diversity of sizes, shapes and behaviors in the feathered kingdom. This diversity represents an almost endless opportunity for viewing pleasure.

And it seems only natural that we should be attracted to and fascinated by birds; there's something reassuring and comforting about their presence. Maybe it's because where there are no birds, there's little hope for man. A coal mine that won't support a canary is, of course, unfit for the miner. The weary sailor knows that a bird overhead means land close by. With a few exceptions, birds are generally good omens, and their absence a warning.

But watching them—the art and science of birding— doesn't have to mean tromping through some boggy backwoods marsh with a full kit, heavy guidebook, expensive spotting glasses and checklist. You can experience every bit as much enjoyment by observing a diversity of windborne wildlife in your own backyard—as long as you're willing to take some basic steps toward creating an inviting, bird-friendly locale.

Fortunately, a welcoming environment for birds looks roughly the same as a rich garden landscape. Start with a healthy diversity of plants, creating a wealth of blooms and drawing different types of insects. There should also be a good water feature, as formal as a birdbath or as integrated and natural as a pond in a corner of the garden. A food source that rounds out what they'll find among the plants will also make your yard more attractive to winged visitors. Lastly, if you want birds to extend their stay you should provide them living quarters suited to the way they nest and protected from potential predators and nuisances. This book offers advice on all this, helping you tempt birds with a destination that will seem like avian paradise.

We've provided information on all the basics—food, lodging, comfort and protection—in the chapters that follow. You'll find great projects for building classic birdhouses that accommodate different species. All you need do is choose the structure or structures that serve your favorite species and whose design best complements your yard, and then follow the instructions. Many of these designs can even be altered to suit your tastes or to serve a greater range of species. So whether you want to create a vacation stopover for a bluebird or lure in a wren, you'll find the perfect abode in these pages.

Of course, any welcoming spot includes plenty to eat. Birdseed and suet need to be placed where birds can reach them but other animals cannot, or in feeders that prevent larger birds such as pigeons from cadging the supplies of smaller hungry eaters. That's why we've included all manner of bird feeders offering, so to speak, something for every appetite. We've also spelled out the best types of food for different birds in different seasons.

Lastly, few birds can resist a refreshing splash in the water—it's essentially a bird's version of a spa. A good water source not only supplies a place to frolic and bathe, it also offers a cool drink, which is why many birds consider a water feature essential to even a short-term layover. In addition, a water feature—from an oversized water dish to a full-blown multi-tier fountain—can be a lovely decorative accent to your garden. You'll find some very interesting and attractive versions in the chapters that follow.

Once you've supplied the water, food and quarters, the birds are sure to come; then it's just a matter of enjoying them. To take advantage of all the fun birding offers, you'll need a few basic tools. A reputable identification guide is an excellent addition to the porch or patio you use for watching birds. You'll find many authoritative guides on the bookstore shelf; just be sure the guide covers your region of the country.

You should also invest in a decent pair of binoculars, because really enjoying the activities, colors and markings of birds means watching them up close (something that is a little hard to do without scaring the creatures away). To help you find just the right binoculars for you and your viewing conditions, we've included a chapter that introduces these essential birding tools. You'll find a simple description of the factors that separate different models and styles of binoculars, with specific recommendations for what works best for the novice and backyard birder.

We've also included in-depth information about how the seasons affect bird-watching and what to expect from birds when nesting, migrating or just grabbing a bite to eat in your backyard.

The only other "tools" you absolutely must have are a little patience and attentiveness, which will pay great dividends as the endlessly interesting world of birds becomes yours to explore.

CHAPTER 1

SPRING AND SUMMER

Spring and summer are the prime seasons for bird-watching. Not only are these the most pleasant seasons for you to enjoy time outdoors; as migratory birds return home, they flood your yard with hungry, active characters. Love is in the air. Showy males strut their stuff, sing their songs and stake their claims. Pairs enter into genetically programmed mating rituals, build nests and lay their eggs. The spectacle of life begins anew as young birds learn to hunt and try their first flight, putting on a show that you surely don't want to miss. These are the best times to be a bird, and to be a bird-watcher.

THE SPRING EXODUS

As the northern weather warms and the days begin to lengthen, migratory birds make their way home in droves. This reverse migration presents great opportunities for observing birds you might not otherwise get a chance to see. As birds make their way to their breeding grounds, they make frequent stopovers along the way, taking advantage of landscapes that are blooming with life and food sources. If you've planted a diverse garden, it will pay big dividends, attracting many of these travelers to your yard. Be ready with your binoculars and you'll be treated to a multicolored and varied show.

For instance, warblers who made long trips down to Central and South America make their way back up north in spring. Sporting beautiful colors, these little travelers stop to take advantage of a quickly

ADVICE FROM A BIRDER If you come across a bird that has flown into a window and appears to be dead, don't touch it. The bird is likely simply stunned and will recover if left alone. Instead, keep an eye out for potential predators until the bird is well enough to fly away on its own.

AIR SHOW

Raptors such as hawks return to nesting sites in spring and along the way, some will put on amazing aerial displays. Riding air currents to conserve energy, these birds can seem as graceful as dancers. But the real fireworks begin with their mating rituals, when the males, and sometimes the females as well, put on stunning shows of amazingly choreographed dives and flying. If you're close to raptors' nesting areas, the show is well worth catching in mid to late spring.

escalating insect population, often passing through grouped in large flocks. Keep an eye out because you may just find a wave of these little wayfarers—sometimes many different species wearing showy sunburst yellows and deep blacks—brightening your yard in early spring. These birds even stop over in cities, where they take advantage of large parks. They use the green oases as a place to safely rest, to dine on vegetation and insects and to enjoy any significant body of water. Even if you live in a well-tended suburban development, you might get a chance to see a short-tailed flycatcher up close and personal—even though the bird usually lives in the wilder confines of a marshy retreat.

But birds in transit aren't the only ones populating your yard in spring. This is the time for overwintering

resident birds to come out from their protected roosts, stake out their territory and begin the process of mating and nesting that they've waited so long for.

As you watch the numbers of birds grow and fill your yard with chatter and frantic movement, probably the first thing you'll notice are all the lovely colors. After winter's drab palette, birds that molt will put on their vivid mating coats, growing new and stunning feathered garments. For instance, the male goldfinch changes his uninspiring olive drab winter wear for a brilliant gold set of feathers with a pure ebony hood. The scarlet tanager will experience a partial molt resulting in his spectacular crimson body.

THE BIRD-WATCHING GARDENER

You can take advantage of early spring to make your yard even more inviting to the winged locals. When planning out your garden—especially if you're making new plantings—select a mix of plants that will create

three seasons of blooms, or shrubs that produce berries throughout the summer and into fall. A mix of evergreen and deciduous trees is also a great combination if your yard can accommodate them.

Many species of plants are particularly appealing to birds or to the insects that, in turn, attract birds. Abelia is a favorite shrub for butterflies and hummingbirds and

ADVICE FROM A BIRDER Beginning backyard birders can easily become overwhelmed by trying to use a field guide to identify the many birds that move through the garden in spring. Don't get too caught up in immediately trying to identify the birds you see. Your first step should just be to become familiar with the birds in your yard. Focus on color, size and features such as beak shape. Note these in a journal and over time, as you come to recognize the birds you see repeatedly, you will be able to find them from memory in a field guide.

BIRDHOUSE SPANS HIGH POST OF GARDEN GATE

Instead of just a plain tie strip across two high posts supporting a gate to his garden, one homeowner mounted a long birdhouse on top of the strip. Simple in construction, the house has four nesting compartments, one at each end and two in the center. Two gables and a false chimney at the center break up the plain lines of the house and give it a more realistic touch. Screws through the tie strip and house bottom hold it in place.

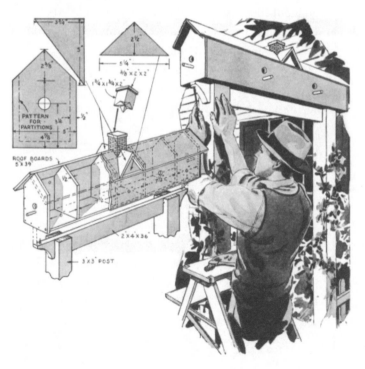

provides good cover for other birds. Hollyhock is a similar attraction for hummingbirds. American beautyberry will get all kinds of attention from a range of birds because of its purple berries, which last all summer long. Coral berry also attracts the hungry bird, especially because it features berries in winter. Big-bloomed flowers are prized by many birds for the easy treasure of their seed heads. These include cornflowers, coreopsis, dahlias and other flowerbed standards. Flowering trees such as dogwood are also preferred plantings for the bird garden.

As part of your yard chores, you should service bird

feeders, nesting boxes and birdbaths. Birds are susceptible to fungus and other contaminants in their food, so thoroughly clean the feeders that you'll be using over the summer. Use a little bit of bleach in hot water and scrub the feeders thoroughly, allowing them to dry completely before you restock them with food. Before the home-seeking hordes arrive, you should open up any nesting boxes in your yard and clean them as well. If they were well used during the previous season, be sure to return them to exactly the same spot.

Birdbaths require a good spring cleaning as well. Scrub the basin and use bleach to get rid of algae buildup and stains. Again, rinse the bath thoroughly after cleaning, and allow it to dry completely before adding fresh clean water. As nice as your birdbath may be, spring is also the time to consider adding a noisy water feature, such as a

small fountain or a waterfall behind a pond. The sound of splashing water is very inviting to birds, and you may find that its addition increases the number of visitors to your yard. While you're at it, scrub your wire fences clear of old vines to provide new perches for your feathered friends.

merit of blending well with its surroundings and being economical to make. A circular form of old bricks was made about 14 in. high and 2 ft. in diameter at the base, tapering to about 20 in. at the top. The brick form was filled with cinders to within a few inches of the top, leaving a depression that sloped from 5 in. at its deepest point to about $1/2$ in. below the rim. In this way bathing and drinking accommodations are provided for birds of all sizes, from a wren to a flicker. The whole structure is covered with a coat of one part cement to three parts of clean sand. Both the inside of the basin and the exterior are finished rough, and when completed, the wheel has the appearance of a large bowler than harmonizes well with its surroundings.

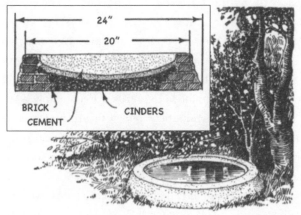

BIRD LOVERS WILL FIND THEMSELVES AMPLY REPAID IN THE SOCIETY AND FRIENDSHIP OF THEIR FEATHERED PALS BY PROVIDING THEM WITH DRINKING AND BATHING FACILITIES.

THE LOOK OF LOVE

In spring, a young man's fancy turns to thoughts of love, and male birds are no different. Most male birds spend their early spring frantically establishing territory and attracting a mate. And those two behaviors are closely tied together, no more so than in the songs birds sing.

Male birds use their songs to say, "This is my territory, so stay out," and "If you're a female, here I am." Although they may sound similar to us, birds are incredibly adept at understanding what these songs mean, and even at determining which particular bird is singing. Songs can serve many purposes; what sounds like a short song, for example, may be a call of warning or a threat.

Common songsters include titmice, sparrows, tree swallows and purple finches. Oddly, a big part of bird-watching is listening. Bird songs are quite distinctive and after paying attention to the sounds of the birds in

DOWN AND DIRTY

Several backyard birds, such as robins and some species of swallows, will use mud to fortify their nests when available. Help them out by creating a small mud puddle in an out-of-the-way corner of your yard. It's a good chance to get a look at these busy birds in action, and if you follow their flights, they will reveal nest locations.

your yard for a short time, you'll begin to differentiate one song from another. In time, you will even be able to tell the calls of different species from one another and possibly even recognize the songs of an individual bird. Although males produce the most songs by far, in some species both males and females have their songs.

Some species don't have a song but still manage to make sounds that clearly define what they consider to be

ADVICE FROM A BIRDER When it comes to birding, your ears can be every bit as valuable as your eyes. Just as you would note the physical characteristics of bird in your backyard, pay attention to the songs you hear. Each bird has a distinctive song, and if you listen closely, you can make out the pattern. Note this pattern in your journal, and after awhile, you'll be able to match the song to the birds you're seeing, and you'll have another way of knowing what birds are present in the yard.

REFLECTING AGGRESSION

The spring season brings with it a rather strange phenomenon that can be disconcerting for both the bird-watcher and the bird. Birds at this time of year quite frequently fly headlong into large windows (and sometimes even the windows and mirrors of cars). The birds can hit the window hard enough to stun and, in some cases, even injure themselves. The same bird will then attack the window again. You're most likely to notice this with robins and some species of sparrows. This behavior has a very simple explanation: The bird is protecting its territory. Birds have exceptional vision but small brains, so they don't know that the reflection they see in window glass isn't another bird. What they see is an interloper, and they fly at the stranger in an effort to scare the invading bird away. Do the male birds in your yard a favor by shielding the reflective image. If you're willing, you can streak the windows with bar soap, which will break up any reflected image. (Take heart: You only have to keep the soap on the windows until the end of the mating season.) As an alternative, you can drape netting in front of the window or put an awning over the window so that it appears black in the bird's field of vision.

their territories, or that a mate will understand as an invitation. Crows have their loud and distinctive (and to our ears, irritating) caw, while woodpeckers "drum" out their messages on trees or the deeply resonating surfaces of drainpipes or even chimneys.

Even once a male has used his gift of sound and attracted a female—and repelled other possible suitors—he hasn't finished with his courtship rituals. In some species, particularly larger birds and birds of prey, both the males and females participate in courtship "shows." But in most backyard birds, it's the male who does most of the showing off, in an effort to strengthen the bond between the pair prior to mating. For instance, the common house swallow puffs up his chest and tilts his head back to display his most colorful part, the underneck bib. Among some swans and ducks, the female will present herself almost like a hungry juvenile, and the male will then showily supply her with a gift of food. Dances or aerial displays are also common ways a male bird exhibits

ADVICE FROM A BIRDER If you're trying to identify the birds in your backyard, you can look for distinctive behaviors. How a bird holds its head to listen for possible predators, how it flies, and peculiar actions like the motions it makes in the presence of a predator are all clues to the species. These are also great ways to get to know the birds in your yard and discover more about them.

his fitness to be a mate. Some skylarks will fly dramatically into the air, executing maneuvers meant to thrill the female and singing his courtship song while he flies.

Observing these courtship rituals makes for some of the most riveting bird-watching, but you should never get close enough to interrupt the process or make loud and obvious movements that might distract the birds.

With the female suitably impressed, it's time for mating—the key event of the spring season. In several

HOLLOW-LOG BIRDHOUSES

Those who delight in watching their feathered friends can use sections of hollow logs to create birdhouses that are far more attractive than almost any kind made of boards.

The type shown in the drawing is made from a length of log mounted on a pole. The piece of log is thoroughly cleaned of all rot and is held in place between the circular bottom platform and the solid top with long bolts, as indicated in the illustration.

The thickness of the walls will be determined to some extent by the amount of sound wood in the interior of the log; if it is too thick, it can be cut down by using a carpenter's gouge.

Holes are drilled through the sides, and the interior may be divided into several compartments by suitable partitions. The most pleasing proportions are obtained with a birdhouse of the type shown, when the section of log forming the body of the house is about 2 in. longer than its diameter. The height of the cap, or top, is not as high as the walls. Such a birdhouse can be mounted on the end of a pole (as shown) or, by putting a screw eye into the center of the cap, suspended from a tree branch. Four alternative log homes are pictured.

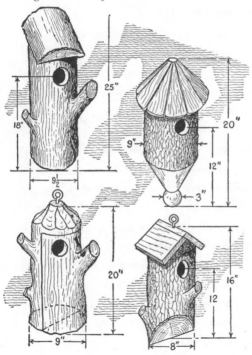

species, mating involves nest building either before or after the actual mating event. In some cases, the pair will work together on the nest, with the male often gathering material and the female constructing the nest itself. In fewer instances, the male will actually construct the nest as a mating gesture. Some species of wrens actually build multiple nests so that the female can choose her favorite. But more often then not, the male is a modest participant in the nest-building exercise.

FINDING THE NEST

The activities of nest building, egg laying, incubation and the raising of the young are some of most interesting bird-watching you'll do. Of course, to see all that, you'll need to have some idea of where the nest is located. A singing male  *usually means his nest is nearby. If you see a pair of birds engaged in an obvious mating ritual, the nest is very close. If a bird is picking up loose material, you can visually follow it to the nest. If a bird flushes every time you walk by a shrub or small tree, there is most likely a nest hidden in the branches or underneath. As much as possible, search at a distance using binoculars. If you get to close to the nest, you may interrupt the nesting and mating processes.*

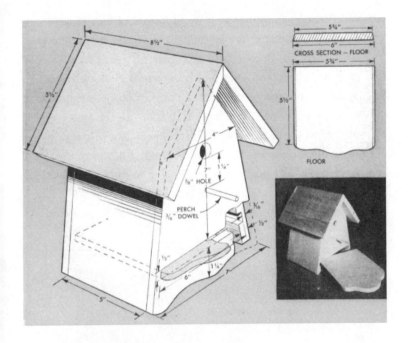

WREN HOUSE FEATURING PULL-OUT FLOOR

Differing primarily in its provision for cleaning, this little wren house, with its pull-out floor, is a natural favorite for any bird-loving homeowner. A few simple jigs to ensure identical parts will permit the home craftsman to create one for himself and others as presents. In addition, there is no bottom to nail into place, which means a shorter assembly time. The dowel perch may be omitted because the projecting floor serves as a built-in ledge.

Some species prefer to squat in other birds' nests—a good argument for watching previously abandoned nest sites for new activity. For instance, you may see bluebirds, tree swallows and some wrens gladly take up lodgings in empty woodpecker holes or other tree cavities. Certain species of owls will, too. In fact, you can often find birds' nests in dead trees or hollowed-out portions of living ones. However, the vast majority of birds craft their own home in a location that suits their own particular needs. These needs are primarily related to safety. Although any bird wants to nest close to a food

ADVICE FROM A BIRDER If you hope to see the full range of bird activity in your yard, especially around breeding time, follow this rule: Hands off! If you get to close to breeding birds, they may become stressed and frightened, and in some cases may even abandon the nest with eggs or defenseless hatchlings inside. For the same reason, don't touch any nests or chicks you come across. Even if you think a bird is in distress, leave it alone. A fledgling that is on the ground rather than in the nest may be learning to fly, and the parents may well be watching over it. Always keep in mind that you're just the audience—not an actor.

THE TENANT

The cuckoo is one of a limited group of species that uses other birds' nests to lay its eggs. A peculiar adaptation to this tendency for squatting rather than building is that the cuckoo will usually lay only one egg in the borrowed nest (risking as little as possible in the event its encroachment is discovered). The egg the cuckoo lays also often mimics the coloration of the host's eggs.

source, they all will focus on a location that provides the best security for vulnerable eggs and hatchlings. This means a location that is either hidden from view or extremely difficult to reach for nonwinged enemies. And birds—especially otherwise vulnerable ground-dwelling species—are exceptional at camouflaging their nests, making them difficult to detect.

If you keep your eyes open, you're likely to find nest locations varying from messy undergrowth or secluded trees that builders of cup-shaped nests such as thrushes call home. But birds are also amazingly adept at creating a home in the most obscure and unwelcoming places,

WREN HOUSE FROM AUTO CASING

Jenny wren will appreciate this little house, which is nothing more than a short piece of auto casing fitted with wood ends cut to shape and nailed in place. A 1-in. hole bored in one end serves as a door, and a board nailed to the bottom of the old casing and to the ends provides a base for this little house.

such as the crag faces on which hawks build their nests. So when you're searching for nests in your yard, look high and low—and everywhere in between.

What constitutes a nest also varies from species to species. A few birds lay their eggs on bare ground, but most go to the effort of at least putting together a rudimentary structure, even if they are a ground-dwelling species. Don't discount what first appears to be a pile of leaves and twigs: A depression may be a quail's nest, or that of the short-eared owl—they lay on trampled undergrowth. Higher up, many types of birds (including redwings and blue jays) make modest bowl-shaped nests out of collections of twigs, salvaged bits of twine, moss and lichen, feathers or other materials—including, in many cases, their own saliva. Crows nest in the open, as high in a tree as they can possibly build, so that even though the nest is exposed, it's not accessible to predators. If you're

CLAY FLOWERPOTS USED FOR BIRDHOUSES

The common garden flowerpot can be turned into a novel birdhouse by enlarging the small opening at the bottom with a pair of pliers and carefully breaking the clay away until the opening is large enough for a small bird.

Place the pot upside down on a board 3 in. wider than the diameter of the largest pot used. Fasten it to the board with wood cleats and brass screws. Fit the cleats as close as possible to the sides of the pot. One or more pots may be used, as shown in the sketch.

The board on which the pots are fastened is nailed or screwed to a post or pole 10 or 12 ft. in height. The board is braced with lath or similar strips of wood, making a framework suitable for a roost. In designing the roost, the lath can be arranged to make it quite attractive, or the braces can be made of twigs and tree branches to create a rustic effect.

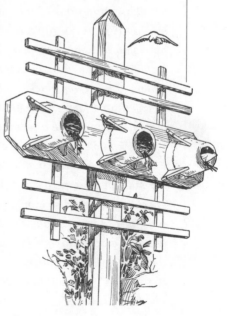

ever lucky enough to see a bald eagle nest, you'll witness the master of nest builders at its craft; they may take up to three months to finish a nest, and the final structure can be as large as 6 ft. deep and 15 ft. in diameter.

Once the female's eggs are fertilized and she settles down in preparation for the laying process, the two birds assume their parental roles. Because the female is using much of her energy to produce the eggs, the male

A NARROW ESCAPE

One of the first difficulties a hatchling must face is actually getting out of the egg. Given that the egg-shell is a pretty durable and tough coating and the hatchling has undeveloped muscles, this is more of a challenge than it might appear. Fortunately, nature equips the young chick with a couple of specialized features for making its escape—and that make watching the escape a riveting event. Each chick has what's known as an egg tooth, a sharp growth from the upper beak area meant specifically for breaking the shell (it disappears shortly after hatching) and a specialized, fast-developing neck muscle that allows the chick to bang against the shell repeatedly. Once you see cracks appear in the shell, keep an eye on the egg to follow the progress of the little bird as it uses its unusual tools to escape its no-longer-needed sanctuary.

will aid her in food gathering. Finally, she lays the eggs and the period of incubation begins. This is a time near the end of the spring when the garden, and the local environment at large, is flourishing with life. Flowers, berries and early fruit and seed sources are popping out all over. The insect population is booming. Biologically, the laying time has largely been predetermined to take advantage of this bounty. As the eggs hatch and noisy hatchlings call out for food almost incessantly (they feed every 15 to 20 minutes on average), the parents can rely on abundant sources of nutrition. You'll have many, many opportunities to see parents in action during this season.

Even birds that are largely seed eaters or vegetarians will begin to look for sources of protein to feed their young. Hatchlings will grow at an amazing rate through the spring and summer months, and that growth is fueled by protein such as worms and grubs.

THE SUMMER ROUTINE

As spring turns to summer, birds become quieter because their territories have been established and their mates chosen. The songbirds still sing, but less intensely. Watching the scene from your backyard, you'll see plenty of activity in area nests as hatchlings mature quickly, growing downy, messy feathers if they didn't have them already and attempting to move around as their muscles grow. In most pairs, the parents will be working together to feed the hungry young ones, and finding food will become the major occupation of the birds in your yard as summer progresses. Of course, they will still tend to other necessary functions, such as bathing, so it's essential to keep a clean source of water at the ready for them.

All young birds quickly develop a set of juvenile feathers and grow the physical features that will allow them to evade predators and gather food. Watch for this process—the more quickly the juvenile can develop these attributes, the less time the bird spends as a prisoner of the nest and a potential target for predators. You can tell the juveniles by their scruffy appearance, a result of the speed at which nestlings grow their first set of feathers. The feathers are imperfect—like baby teeth— and you'll see most birds replace that first set within a few months through a process called molting. You can usually detect juveniles not only by these untidy first feathers, but also by markings that are similar in nature and color to those of the adult bird, only more haphazard and less distinct.

You'll see an advantage to the disheveled appearance many juveniles' markings give them when they leave the nest. Less pronounced markings allow them to blend more easily into a protective thicket of leaves and branches or tangled undergrowth.

Pay attention day to day, because young nestlings grow rapidly. There are plenty of photo ops as these hungry, down-covered or naked creatures feed almost constantly and gain weight at a fevered pace. Usually, within two weeks the hatchlings' first set of feathers has come in (although not necessarily grown in all the way). Within a month, the birds are almost as heavy or

even heavier than their parents, and they are ready to leave the nest (in a process called fledging). You can judge the rate of maturation by comparing the size of the hatchlings with the size of their parents and siblings. The process may not seem all that fast, but the truth is that hatchlings are genetically programmed to mature and leave the nest as quickly as possible.

Leaving the nest inevitably means flying—except in flightless species, which you're not likely to encounter in the backyard! There is a general misconception that the parent bird teaches its young to fly, but even the most casual observation will put the lie to that idea. All young birds of a species that does fly are preprogrammed to fly. They have the knowledge; they just need a skeletal structure and muscles strong enough to propel them through the air. It makes for some exciting and often amusing bird-watching when the mother bird prods a reluctant juvenile out of the nest. But that's not flight instruction.

It's simply a timer programmed in the adult to make sure the young bird progresses to the next stage, ensuring survival.

All young birds, whether fliers or not, share the inevitability of having to leave the nest and become fledglings. If they learn to forage effectively and evade predators—and have a little bit of luck—they'll become adults.

Of course, there will also be instances in which the adults still needs to protect their young from predators, both airborne and not. This is a great time for some behavioral bird-watching. You might see blue jay fledglings bumble about or doing nothing at all while the mother bird unearths grubs and other protein sources for the hapless youth. You'll surely see some flying misadventures. Although juvenile birds are programmed to fly and don't need their parents to teach them, that doesn't mean that they can fly well or make good directional decisions. You may well get the chance to see some rather comical incidents involving these inexperienced fliers, including overshooting landing sites, flying into solid objects and even crashing into other birds.

The young birds' skills increase as summer wanes. Although they won't necessarily be as adept at gathering food, flying or nesting as their parents are, by the end of the summer these young birds will be able to feed themselves, avoid predators (to a greater or lesser degree) and navigate their environment.

You should be able to track the juveniles in your yard because their coloring will still be different from the adult birds'. In fact, it may take up to two years for the juveniles of some species to grow feathers in typical adult colors.

END OF SUMMER AND PACKING THE BAGS

August is the time that many birds begin molting or partially molting a new, duller set of feathers. Most birds also begin to ramp up their food consumption as a first step toward packing on the extra fat they'll need for winter. And although the end of the summer is usually a time of preparation, some early migrators start their trips to their cold weather homes. Around the end of August, swallows will begin to flock together, forming the groups they'll use for additional protection and food gathering during the trip south. They are joined by certain species of warblers that don't want to wait for the first chill before leaving their summer haunts.

These early departures are the first signs of impending fall. Pay close attention and you'll notice them as flocks heading south or visitors to your garden you don't usually see there.

CHAPTER 2

FALL AND WINTER

T he fall and winter brings new potential for seeing birds you might not usually see in your yard. The colder months are a time of transition for all species of bird. For some, the change in weather means preparing for and flying long journeys to more hospitable climates. To others—the permanent residents—it means hunkering down and finding friends and shelter in order to survive the harsher weather to come. But regardless of what type of bird visits your yard— the local resident looking to stay the winter or the traveler making a stopover—there is still activity to be seen in the last months of the year.

AUTUMN'S CHANGES

F all is your chance to attract many birds to your yard to feed. Because birds in fall are looking to bulk up regardless of whether or not they are migrating, they take advantage of any available food source, particularly as the insect and fruit populations begin to dwindle. Fill your feeders with oily, fat- and protein-rich seeds, the best possible aid for birds looking to gain crucial weight. For instance, small northern birds will need to increase their weight 10 percent or more on average to safely make it through the cold times to come. A wonderful choice for birds as varied as blue jays, goldfinches and nuthatches is black sunflower seeds (sometimes called oil seeds). Safflower is also a nutritious choice, although it is an acquired taste and has a more limited audience, being a food of choice for titmice, cardinals and some woodpeckers. Squirrels don't like it, so it's a good selection for exposed feeders that might otherwise fall prey to these bushy-tailed bandits.

THE BULK-UP DIET

Suet, a mix of animal fat rendered with seeds and other fillers, is the ideal fall and winter food for birds. The high fat content gives birds a chance to quickly bulk up and fuels the energy they will expand in making long migratory flights or surviving the cold over winter if they don't migrate.

ADVICE FROM A BIRDER It may be a natural inclination when clearing up yard debris in late fall to remove nests from leafless trees, but fight your clean-up urges. Although most birds will look to build new nests in the spring, some will return to nests they built the year before, and others, such as nuthatches, will gladly inhabit nests built and abandoned by other birds.

You can also help your local bird population by letting your garden go a bit. Plants that have gone to seed and died, and even flowers that remain uncut and withered on the stalk, will serve as valuable food sources as the winter turns cold. A thickly vegetated, diverse garden may even offer food stock well into winter, helping those birds who don't migrate.

If you're watchful and regularly note the birds in your backyard, it's likely you'll notice some other subtle changes in the bird population even before certain groups take off for their semiannual migration. One of the most notable of these changes is new plumage. As male birds molt, they will replace their flashier feathers with less colorful clothes because they no longer need bright colors to attract a mate and duller shades are less likely to be noticed by predators. At this point, in many species, the male will closely resemble the female.

Fall also marks a change in the singing patterns of most birds. Some will quit singing altogether, while

WINTER FEEDERS

As winter closes in, make sure that your feathered friends will not be forgotten when snow and ice make food scarce. By getting an early start in making either one of the two attractive feeders pictured and detailed in the accompanying illustrations, you'll be ready to offer a handout when the snow begins to fall.

The hopper-type feeder shown at left is built around a washbasin and a chimney taken from an

HOPPER-TYPE FEEDER

WASHBASIN

SOLDERED

LAMP CHIMNEY

RUBBER WASHER

¼" ROD

METAL CHIMNEY HOLDER

HANGING FEEDER

SOLDERED

¼"

⅜" DOWEL

TURNED FROM 2" X 6" STOCK

old kerosene lamp. The chimney holds a supply of birdseed that works down onto a turned wooden feeding tray. To replenish the seed, the basin is removed by unscrewing the hanger nut at the top. The tray, chimney, washbasin and sheet-metal chimney holder are all held together with a ¼-in. rod that runs through the center of the feeder. In windy localities, the vane-type feeder shown affords welcome shelter from wintry blasts because the plywood trees serve as vanes that always keep the back of the

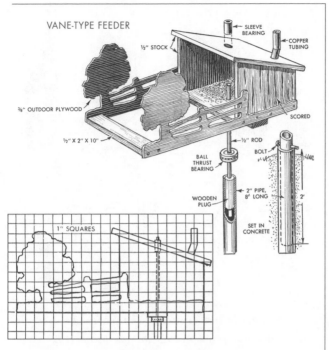

VANE-TYPE FEEDER

SLEEVE BEARING

COPPER TUBING

½" STOCK

⅜" OUTDOOR PLYWOOD

SCORED

½" X 2" X 10"

½" ROD

BALL THRUST BEARING

BOLT

WOODEN PLUG

2" PIPE, 8' LONG

2'

SET IN CONCRETE

1" SQUARES

feeder to the wind. Resting on a ball thrust bearing, the feeder turns freely even in a light breeze. Note how the rod on which the feeder pivots is fitted in the upper end of the pipe standard. A wooden plug drilled slightly undersize for the ¹/₂-in. rod is turned a little oversize for a drive fit in the pipe. Many species of birds, especially those that remain during the winter, are very fond of suet. A convenient method of offering this food is to bore a few 1-in. holes in a stick of firewood, add a decorative thatched roof and fill the holes with it.

continued on next page

continued from previous page

NESTING SHELF

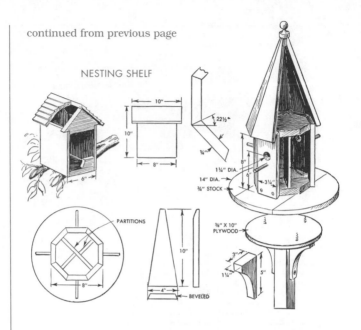

Songbirds that winter in the warm climates and have no food problem are always in need of homes and nesting boxes, and the ones pictured will provide desirable housing. The simple nesting shelf shown below will find favor among robins, phoebes and purple martins. These birds require houses with one side open and a roomy floor area. The octagonal four-compartment house is suitable for the wren, chickadee, nuthatch, titmouse and the downy woodpecker. If only one partition is installed, making two compartments instead of four, and the entrance enlarged from 7/8 in. to 1 1/2 in., the house will accommodate bluebirds,

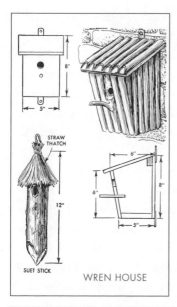

tree swallows or violet-green swallows. Note that the walls of the house are screwed to the floor to facilitate cleaning. The rustic wren house shown is made by covering a boxlike unit with split twigs; the back is fastened with screws to make it easier to clean. A $^7/_8$-in. bit is used to bore the entrance hole in the house.

WREN HOUSE

other birds will sing at different times and usually, for different reasons. Whereas the songs of spring are used for many different purposes—mating calls, territorial markers and other communications—the tunes in fall are primarily used to warn other birds away from food sources or as succinct messages for birds seeking the protection of a flock. The mockingbird is an example of a bird that keeps its distinctive triple-cadence song despite the cold weather. The mourning dove will use its cooing to instruct other members of the flock about where to roost and a more excited call in the presence of a potential predator.

The waning light of the cold seasons initiates other changes in birds' bodies that spur them to prepare for travel. They're also responding to a decline in food stores (although you needn't worry about leaving feeders out: They won't sway a migrating species from taking off as planned). Over fall, migrating species will look to bulk up to ensure they have enough fat supplies to make their

---

THE BIRDS OF HALLOWEEN

Fair or not, certain birds carry with them reputations for creepy and even supernatural behaviors—especially tied to that end-of-harvest fall holiday, Halloween. Consider the raven. Having starred in the classic spooky Edgar Allan Poe poem, this sleek and shiny black bird seems designed for All Hallows Eve. The crow is even more of a frightful apparition, with its loud and disconcerting cry. Add to that the Native American myth that the bird carried the souls of the dead to purgatory, and this becomes one of the eeriest birds around. Vultures are a natural Halloween villain, with their ugly, menacing appearance and their culinary desire for dead flesh. Last but not least are owls. The barn owl is a stage prop in many a horror movie. This otherwise attractive bird features a hair-raising call that is somewhere between a scream and cry. It also makes for a chilling site in a graveyard at night, with its white underwings and tail giving it a ghostly appearance.

journey. This means that as millions of birds make their ways to new climates, they present opportunities to view species you may not regularly see in your yard.

BIRD-WATCHING DURING MIGRATION

Depending on where you live, migrating birds will begin their trips in mid fall to early winter. One morning you may wake up to find that the leaves have changed color and many of the birds in your backyard have simply disappeared. But even if you live in the north, you'll probably get a chance to see a variety of tired feathered travelers stopping by for a day or two to rest and eat what they can find (another good reason to keep your bird feeders stocked right through winter!). For instance, tree swallows make their way south from New England right down the eastern seaboard. They stop frequently along the way for a little rest and to enjoy late-season bayberries or similar treats.

If you look to the skies, you'll see traditional migrations, such as the classic V-formation of Canadian geese, along with flocks of ducks and a few other birds. You will also see other daytime migrants, such as loons, crows, cowbirds, swifts, hawks and gulls. However, don't limit your sky watching to the daytime. Many birds prefer to fly in migration at night to avoid predators. These include cuckoos, short-tailed flycatchers, vireos, warblers and orioles. If the moon is full and the sky is clear, a little nighttime sky gazing might just net you a view of some unusual flocks heading south. You can enhance the experience with a modest telescope or a powerful

ADVICE FROM A BIRDER Rescuing an injured bird can be tricky. First and foremost make sure you have somewhere to take the bird—many veterinarians will not treat small birds. Contact your local wildlife center to get help. Then wrap the bird securely in a towel. Don't be rough, but be firm, because the bird is sure to struggle. Pin its wings and feet to its body, and wrap its head as well, leaving just enough room for it to breathe. Transport the bird in a wood, cardboard or plastic box equipped with breathing holes.

spotting scope, using the moon as a background light source to view the birds' silhouettes. Migrating birds typically fly below 6,000 ft., but some species have been known to go higher than 30,000 ft. in an effort to cross over a mountain range.

If you don't think you are in a migration alley, think again. Surprisingly, birds do not always migrate from north to south. Some birds will actually migrate further north to preferred wintering grounds. Others may travel later- ally. For instance, if you live at the base of a mountain or mountain range, keep an eye out for winter tourists. Certain high-altitude birds, such as chickadees, rosy- finches and pine grosbeaks, will migrate down below the snow line in the mountains, wintering in areas that are still cold, but not frozen. What's more, many birds skirt large bodies of water, flying around them and offering

BIRD CAFETERIA

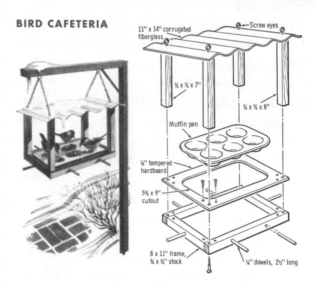

11" x 14" corrugated fiberglass

Screw eyes

¾ x ¾ x 7"

¾ x ¾ x 8"

Muffin pan

⅛" tempered hardboard

5¾ x 9" cutout

8 x 11" frame, ¾ x ¾" stock

¼" dowels, 2½" long

Whether you hang it from a bracket outside a window or from a pole in the yard, this economical bird feeder will give bird-watchers hours of winter pleasure. The key to the whole design, of course, is the use of a low-cost muffin tin to provide a half dozen separate feeding cups that can be filled with a smorgasbord of different treats to suit any bird's taste.

Dimensions listed in the drawing below are designed to accommodate a specific six-cup muffin pan. However, the cutout in the hardboard platform must fit the cup area of the pan you use, so check this carefully before you begin cutting. If you wish to use an eight- or twelve-cup tin, simply enlarge the platform accordingly. But don't change the length of the uprights.

Fasten the platform to the framing strips with countersunk flathead wood screws. Then fasten the uprights to the frame. The screw eyes used to secure the corrugated fiberglass roof to the uprights do double duty as anchors for the 12-in. lengths of chain used to hang the feeder. Give it a coat of paint, fill it with goodies and watch the fun.

bird-watchers on the fringes an impressive viewing opportunity. An example of this is the path of the broad-winged hawk which, in skirting Lake Superior, often gives enthusiasts in areas of Minnesota a glance at a fearsome predator on the wing.

Most, however, will take some variation of a north-to-south route, and migrating birds tend to follow the same path year after year. If you notice some favorites visiting your yard, note the date and a keep an eye out for them around the same time the following year.

By the time the northern winter arrives in full force, bird populations will be largely redistributed. Between December and April, many birds will travel to the southern states. Even more birds travel all the way to Central or South America. However, whether you live in Maine or Florida, Washington State or the heart of Texas, there will still be some terrific bird-watching in winter. If you're in a northern state you'll have fewer varieties to observe, but the birds that are there should be easier to see in the seasonally stripped surroundings.

PERMANENT RESIDENTS

Winter bird-watching in the north or Midwest means looking in different places to find interesting subjects. You can plant your garden to accommodate overwintering birds. In addition to a few coneflowers left to seed in the garden, you can select certain plants, such as some viburnums, that actually maintain berries throughout the winter months. You can also select dense evergreen trees and shrubs for your yard. These will provide cold- and wind-resistant hideouts for overwintering birds and can consequently provide an aviary show if planted in view of a picture window.

At this time of year, birds will roost socially, gathering as a group to aid in finding food, being alert to predators and keeping warm. Common house sparrows will cluster under eaves, chattering away. Walls with thick coverings of ivy or other dense, climbing vines

ADVICE FROM A BIRDER Winter birding can be enjoyable as long as you take precautions to be comfortable while you do it. Even if you're just going out in the backyard, dress in layers so that you can take off clothing if you get too warm. If you're going to watch birds along the shore of a body of water, expect the temperature to be 10 degrees cooler than in your yard.

THE WINTER COAT

Some winter resident birds—those that stay home for winter—adapt to the adverse weather by growing a heavier plumage for increased insulation from the cold. Species that show this trait include ptarmigan, some species of jays and owls, and some types of sparrows. See if you notice changes in the winter birds in you yard; they may be wearing a whole different winter wardrobe!

may be taken as a winter hideaway for dozens of nuthatches, while large tree cavities may house groups of robins or finches.

Some birds, such as crows, blackbirds and starlings, will cluster inside dense evergreens, huddling together to share body heat. These gatherings can number in the thousands and are a protective mechanism against the cold of winter. You can encourage overwintering birds to stay in your yard by building a simple wind-breaking lean-to from small branches and other yard debris.

Winter is also a time many city dwellers can take advantage of seasonal bird-watching. Many overwintering birds find refuge in cities, where they take advantage of the wealth of sheltered structures and a lack of predators.

In cold weather a bird can fluff up its coat to almost twice its natural size, greatly increasing the insulating air spaces between the feathers and creating a wonderful

FREE LUNCH

Providing abundant free lunches by means of a feeder will ensure the health of those birds that remain with you all winter. Feed scattered on the ground not only brings the birds down  *where they are easy prey for cats, but is wasteful and invites rodents as well. The two types of feeders shown will serve most birds that remain during winter. The weather vane type is an all-purpose feeder that rotates so that the open end is always away from the wind. The windowsill type was made primarily for cardinals.*

The sill-type feeder, Figure 1, is nothing more than a glass-paneled box open on one side, with a sloped top and a wood bottom. On the weather vane feeder,

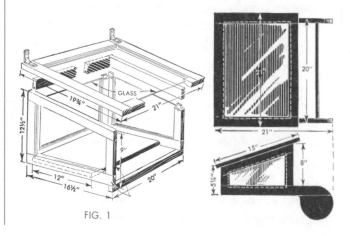

FIG. 1

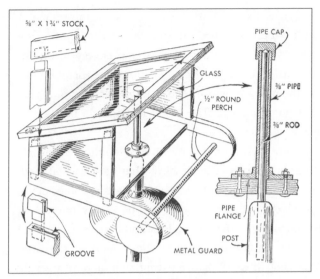

FIG. 3

which is of similar size and shape, the vanes are glued to the underside of the bottom members as indicated in Figure 2. It is best not to extend the bottom of either feeder beyond the glass top because any projection beyond the top will catch the snow.

The weather vane feeder is set on a post that has a pointed rod in the upper end. This fits into a pipe assembly attached to the bottom of the feeder, as in Figure 3, and is located so that the feeder balances on the rod. The pointed end of the rod resting in a shallow countersunk hole in the pipe cap provides a needle-point bearing. Cats and other climbing animals are kept from the feeder by a metal guard.

down jacket for the bird. It's quite a sight to see one of these puffballs perched on an interior section of a tree on a cold December day. If you look closely at one of these birds, you'll see that they also have the ability to tuck their heads within the feathered space and pull their legs up as well. The result looks like a bird left in the clothes drier too long.

Another aspect of winter bird-watching involves following the actions of those birds that have cached food. Nutcrackers, titmice, chickadees and jays are some of the bird world's hoarders, and it can be a very interesting pastime to watch the birds check and make a withdrawal from the various caches they have hidden. Research shows that these birds are exceptional at remembering where the food stashes are, and even what type of food

A CASE OF THE SHIVERS

Birds don't usually shiver; that's an idiosyncrasy normally reserved for less well-outfitted warm-blooded animals. As birds move rapidly around they tend to generate enough muscle warmth to keep the chill away for quite awhile. However, in extreme temperatures you may see birds in somewhat exposed roosts in your yard be overcome by slightly comical bursts of shivering. This is the bird's way of quickly generating muscle warmth (it allows them to increase their metabolic rate as much as five times over normal) and yet another way overwintering birds adapt to the cold.

ADVICE FROM A BIRDER If you're having trouble identifying winter birds in your region, chances are you need a
different guide. Winter is the time to see unusual specimens
such as the snowy owls, Lapland longspurs and golden-crown
sparrows that fly south from Canada. If you live near mountains, expect to see birds that usually live at higher elevations,
such as the varied thrush and mountain chickadee.

they have stashed in which cache. Once you've noted
where the caches are, you'll be able to stake them out
and watch the bird activity there on a fairly regular
schedule (or until the cache is empty). Depending on the
species, a given bird may have dozens of cache sites it
regularly visits.

In colder regions, you can serve the local resident
bird population by continuing to put out high-quality bird
food and water that is not frozen over. If you're willing
to go to the trouble and expense, heated birdbaths are a
real luxury for the wintering bird.

THE DESTINATION SPOTS

If your home is in the South, or even on the West Coast,
you'll have a greater number of bird-watching subjects
from which to choose over the winter months. Certain
areas are the targets of some very interesting mass
migrations. For instance, Rockport, Texas, is a migratory

WINTER SNACK SHACKS
FOR BIRDS

Provide feeding shelters for birds in winter, when snow and sleet seal up their natural food supply, and they will reward you by becoming quite tame and interesting subjects for study and observation. The shelter illustrated is pivoted on a post and swings around in the breeze so that the food will not blow away.

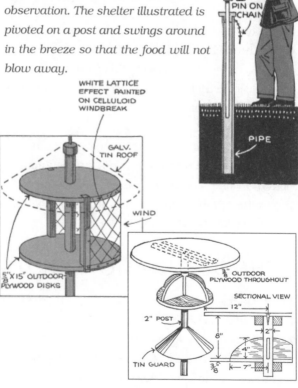

PIPE (GALV.)

PIN ON CHAIN

PIPE

WHITE LATTICE EFFECT PAINTED ON CELLULOID WINDBREAK

GALV. TIN ROOF

WIND

⅝" X 15" OUTDOOR PLYWOOD DISKS

⅜" OUTDOOR PLYWOOD THROUGHOUT

SECTIONAL VIEW

12"

2" POST

8"

2"

4"

⅜"

7"

TIN GUARD

A sliding feeder suspended from a line as shown below can be moved a little closer to the house each day so that you can observe the habits and antics of the birds at close range. A sheaf of grain on a pole is also a welcome sight to snowbound birds.

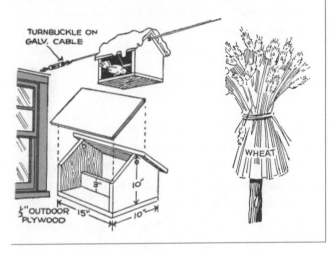

hot spot for ruby-throated hummingbirds, a spectacular sight en masse. They can be found enjoying lantana and many of the region's other flora. Yards in this area just east of Corpus Christi are flooded by the tiny gem-colored birds during the winter holidays. You're likely to see many migrating birds—some on their way to Latin America and others making their winter homes in your neighborhood—if you live in any state along the Gulf of Mexico.

But it's a good idea to always keep an eye out for the unusual specimen because birds sometimes lose their

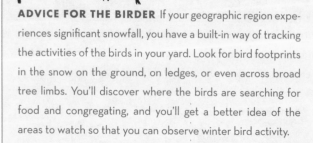

ADVICE FOR THE BIRDER If your geographic region experiences significant snowfall, you have a built-in way of tracking the activities of the birds in your yard. Look for bird footprints in the snow on the ground, on ledges, or even across broad tree limbs. You'll discover where the birds are searching for food and congregating, and you'll get a better idea of the areas to watch so that you can observe winter bird activity.

way in fog or for other reasons. This means you just might encounter a straggler in your own backyard, hundred of miles from where it is supposed to be. Be hospitable and offer it some food and drink while it is there.

Once winter truly sets in, you should make sure that any birds in your yard have a food source with a high fat content and an unfrozen source of fresh, clean water. That will give any birds trying to make it through winter a much better chance of seeing spring's happy sunshine.

CHAPTER 3

GOOD EATING

The types of foods birds eat are as varied as the birds themselves. If you want to observe lots of different birds, you'll need to determine how and what they like to eat. The first step is to understand that there are basically three types of diets among birds: insects, vegetation and larger prey (such as fish or rodents). Most birds will ultimately eat a combination of these diets, depending on changes in the supply of food. In winter, when insects are not readily available, many birds will switch to seeds or other vegetation. The choice of what to eat is mostly determined by nutritional needs or circumstance.

A bird's diet will also vary according to seasonality. A species that prefer a vegetarian diet may switch to hunting insects and oily seeds when feeding their hatchlings and young, which have a greater need for protein than adult birds do. Lastly, they may also change their diet to bulk up for a winter migration.

BIRDS OF PREY

GOLDEN EAGLE

Birds of prey (also called raptors)—eagles, hawks, falcons, kites and owls, among others—put on the most impressive displays of hunting in the bird kingdom, and can make for fascinating watching if you're willing to venture out into the wild (or just to a large local park with wild native landscaping and a significant water feature).

PELLET MAKERS

A key feature among birds of prey, or raptors, is the way they filter out inedible parts of the animals they eat. Raptors have a crop just like more benign birds, such as the pigeon. The crop is used to store food that will be regurgitated and consumed latter, either by the bird itself or by its nestlings. Indigestible parts, such as feathers, hair and certain bones, are collected in the bird's gizzard, where they are mashed up into a ball and later expelled. Raptor trackers can often determine the diet of particular bird by finding and dissecting pellets near a nest. Keep an eye out for pellets on your next nature hike and you may even find the nesting area of a fearsome raptor.

A bird of prey is one that attacks and captures prey with its feet, using a specially shaped beak to tear the creature apart. There are hundreds of types of raptors and they find a place in almost every environment, from the shoreline to the mountains. Although there are some small members of this group (the elf owl measures around 5 in. and can weigh as little as $1^1/2$ oz.) they are generally known for their size, dangerous appearance and remarkable hunting abilities. The largest of these birds, the Andean condor, can grow to 30 lbs., with an awesome wingspan stretching almost 12 ft. across!

This intriguing group of birds is divided by scientists into five different groups, all with their own characteristics and choices of prey. They include: hawks, eagles and kites; vultures and condors; ospreys; falcons and kestrels; and owls. These birds all feature natural equipment well-suited to hunting down game of one sort or another. This group of predators boasts some of the strongest and sharpest talons in the bird world. These birds also have some of the most awe-inspiring flight talents, such as the nearly silent pursuit of a snowy owl on the wing and the spectacular high-speed dive of the peregrine falcon.

Although most birds have extraordinary powers of sight, birds of prey boast visual instruments highly adapted to hunting. For instance, the hawk's focal length allows it to detect small movements of potential targets at great distances.

An owl's eyes are surrounded by specialized feathers that help collect even very small amounts of light, allowing these remarkable nocturnal creatures to pick out a tiny rodent on a moonless night. But that's just one of many

---

DIET OF THE DEAD

Vultures and condors are members of a particularly gruesome bird of prey group—they eat only dead animals, known as carrion. These birds are often large. If you are unsure if you're watching one of these "birds of the underworld" you have only to look at the head. These birds typically have no feathers on their heads— only skin (possibly because they don't want the yucky parts of a corpse sticking to their facial feathers!).

Barn

Screech

Great Horned

TYPES OF OWLS

features that make the owl the most unusual of characters among a highly unusual group of birds. In contrast to most other raptors, the owl hunts primarily at night and relies not only on its exceptional vision but also on some of the best hearing among birds of any kind. An owl's ears (more aural openings than anything else) are—just like its eyes—surrounded by highly specialized feathers that help capture sound waves. The ear tufts on some owls are merely cosmetic; the actual hearing organs are indiscernible. The owl also has a rather creepy ability to seemingly spin its head: the structure of its neck allows it to swivel its head almost three-quarters of the way around.

Other raptors, such as the sparrow hawk, prey on other, smaller birds. But the vast majority of prey birds

Curlew

Yellowlegs   Plover

SHOREBIRDS

hunt smaller mammals and reptiles, such as voles, mice and lizards. Some raptors, such as the eagle, will hunt on both land and water. The eagle is a majestic hunter on open water, where it can plummet at high speed and snatch a fish swimming near the surface. It uses powerful talons to hold the fish firmly, and its strong hooked beak is perfect for tearing the unlucky water dweller apart.

Although not categorized as raptors, a certain group of fearsome feathered hunters focuses almost exclusively on fishing to eat. This is something to keep in mind if you live near a body of water such as lake or even a golf course pond, because fishing birds can put on a good show if you can find somewhere discrete from which to watch them. (They are among the more skittish of birds.) Birds such as kingfishers and herons use their bills to grab fish that swim within striking distance. But while the heron stands and strikes, the kingfisher dives right in. This bird watches the water on high—from a perch in a tree or on a large, tall rock—for signs of its prey. On attack, it flies straight into the water, rising with the fish grasped firmly in its beak. The kingfisher will then stun its lunch by striking the fish against a rock—and then swallow it head first. Quite a scene if you get a chance to see it!

For all their drama, birds of prey are hard subjects for the amateur birder to find and observe. They generally hunt and feed in remote areas, and being larger birds, they require a large territory, making it unlikely that they'll take up residence in your backyard. Also, because they've regularly been hunted by man, this group of birds is even more shy of humans than their smaller cousins. And they are all protected by law.

ADVICE FROM A BIRDER Sometimes it pays to look for the unusual. If you live in the western part of the country near a stream, keep an eye out for the water ouzel, better known as the American dipper. This little round-bodied bird with gray feathers has a unique way of foraging for food. The dipper dives beneath the surface of a stream, swimming below the water in search of larval insects, fish eggs and fish small enough for the diminutive bird to swallow. The bird has even been spied walking on the bottom of a creek in search of a snack.

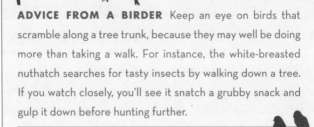
INSECT EATERS

That's why if you're a backyard bird-watcher, you'll probably be focusing on the culinary habits of insect and vegetation eaters. You won't be disappointed; watching how the birds in your yard go about finding a meal can make for some highly amusing and interesting bird-watching.

Although some insect eaters have scooplike beaks that enable them to gather insects on the fly, the more interesting birds to the home enthusiast will be those that forage, dig or poke around for their food. Watching ground feeders such as the thrush can also be very amusing, as they turn over rotting leaves and other natural ground cover in an effort to expose a clutch of worms, grubs or other goodies. Depending on the bird, its efforts can range from a tentative probing to a more comical thrusting aside of leaf litter in what seems like an angry and desperate search for something it has lost. This is why it's a good idea to not rake up all the leaves in your yard. A layer of rotting leaf litter provides a wonderful potential food source for ground-feeding birds.

A greater number of species hunts insects above the ground. Woodpeckers dig out insects from the rotting or damaged wood of trees, and other birds will poke into crevices, cracks and holes in search of a tasty spider or caterpillar. The titmouse will scarf an amazing assortment of bugs and other insects, including ants, wasps and beetles. Wrens are fond of some traditional gardening villains, such as the cutworm and boll weevil, but

---

CHAIRMAN OF THE HOARD

Most birds eat as they go and rely on available food sources. But some are a little bit craftier. Crows are justly famous for their hoarding tendencies. They cache food in different hideouts even when food is plentiful and they may never need the excess. Jays are another species that likes to hide away an edible stash. Jays are particularly fond of acorns, which the birds will collect and hide or bury for consumption much later. This benefits the oak population, because jays do not always make it back to acorns they've buried, and the acorn is moved out of the shade of the parent oak, giving it a better chance of growing into an oak itself.

they will also go after beneficial insects such as bees and spiders. Finches are also good for protecting plants, as they munch on aphids, leaf miners, Japanese beetles and many species of caterpillar—and leave bees alone. Some other birds to watch specifically for their insect-hunting behaviors include chickadees, purple martins, swallows and nuthatches.

ATTRACTING BIRDS WITH FEEDERS

There's nothing like good food to entice visitors to your home. The same is true of your garden. One of the best ways to attract an amazing array of birds to your yard is to offer them easily accessible food. Because their metabolisms are so fast, birds must eat frequently, and they are always on the hunt for nutritious foods as well as any new or bountiful food source. So even if they aren't residents of your yard, birds will visit if they know they can find a reliable free meal.

The trick lies in making the food available to the birds you enjoy while keeping that food away from spoilsports such as squirrels and other, larger birds that have not been invited to the feast. Unfortunately, you can't control which birds decide to join in at mealtime. Even when you supply plentiful food in multiple bird feeders, there will be competition among birds. That's why smart bird-watchers choose feeders that serve the types of birds they want to attract.

TYPES OF FEEDERS

The simplest "bird feeder" is just a scattering of seeds on the ground. This is actually not a bad idea in the cold of winter because it gives ground feeders and other overwintering birds quick access to a meal. But in most all cases you'll want to supplement this rudimentary option with some other, more sophisticated approaches.

PHEASANT FEEDERS FROM MILK CANS KEEP OUT ALL RODENTS

If you have local pheasants or quail on your property and would like to set up a feeder that will not require daily main-tenance, try this ingenious and simple project. Convert an old milk can into a rodent-proof feeder by hammering out air vents and filling the container  *with seed, then string with wire from a low hanging tree branch in your yard.*

ADVICE FROM A BIRDER

Placing a bird feeder in your yard is a great way to get a really good look at the birds that come to eat there, and over time you may notice some oddities. Birds such as house finches may have widely varying colorations depending on their diet, so don't be surprised if the specimen at your feeder doesn't exactly match the description in your guide. In addition, the bird population experiences some genetic abnormalities that can create white or mostly white birds. These are fascinating examples of albinism, the absence of any melanin in the body of the bird. On the other end of the spectrum, you may notice certain birds that are colored much darker than their companions, a result of melanism, or an excess of melanin.

A very simple feeding device is a platform on a pole or standard. Just scatter seed on the platform and you'll have a first-come, first-served cafeteria. Of course, this still gives the edge to larger, more aggressive species. It also presents a challenge in protecting the birds, because pests from squirrels to snakes can often make it up the pole and create quite a different definition for "feeding platform."

You can purchase or make much more sophisticated and specialized feeders. It all comes down to the birds you want to serve. For instance, if you're not fond of pigeons but love finches, you'll want a feeder with tiny perches and small access holes that make it difficult for the larger birds to get at the food or bother the smaller feeders.

Tubular feeders are excellent for just this purpose. Often just a clear tube with small perches, these feeders

---

TWO EASY-TO-MAKE BIRD FEEDERS

Tin cans make fine bird feeders if you don't completely cut off the tops when opening them. Left partly attached, the lids will support dowel perches by rolling the metal around them. The feeder can easily be nailed to the wall of a garage, a wooden garden post or any other structure that will be difficult for cats and other predators to reach.

Another inexpensive and easy-to-make bird feeder can be constructed from a coat hanger. Just pull the hanger out straight until the two wires are parallel, bend the lower end up to form a right-angle projection that is stapled to a perch and wedge a ball of suet between the wires.

can hold a good amount of seed and do not accommodate larger birds. They also blend into the background—perfect if you prefer a feeder that does not steal attention from the garden itself. Smaller birds such as chickadees, nuthatches and goldfinches are especially attracted to this type of feeder, and squirrel baffles are available for most of these units to further ensure that the tiny diners can lunch unmolested.

Of course, you may just want to serve the largest diversity of birds possible, in which case you can buy or build a larger, box-style feeder filled with a generous amount of seed mix.

Other feeders are meant to serve just one type of bird. For instance, finches love thistle seeds and manufacturers have created feeders dedicated to giving finches exactly what they want. The other most common specialized feeder is the hummingbird feeder. These are used to hold and dispense store-bought nectar or a sugar formula created by the home birder. Hummingbird feeders are themselves some of the prettiest for the garden, but if you are a big fan of hummingbirds, be sure to hang more than

AN INNOVATIVE TYPE OF BIRD FEEDER

A hopper-type bird feeder that lets you see the seed supply at a glance can be improvised quickly from a pie plate, lamp chimney, broomstick and wooden cover. The plate is screwed to the lower end of the broomstick after the latter has been drilled through for a smaller dowel on which the chimney rests. A hanging screw eye is driven into the top end of the broomstick and then a wooden cover, drilled to slip over the screw eye and broomstick, is fitted with pieces of half round molding to center the chimney on the cover. To refill the feeder, simply lift off the cover.

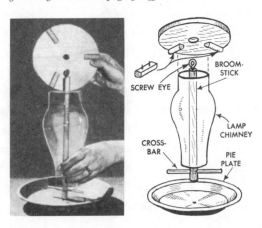

SPLIT KEG PROVIDES BIRD FEEDER

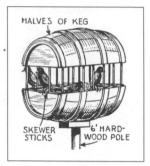

A small keg makes an ideal feeder for birds when it is sawed lengthwise in half through the center. Before sawing the keg, nail the hoops to each stave and nail the ends to keep the assembly from falling apart. Small dowels or skewer sticks are set in holes equally spaced around the edges of each half of the keg to hold them apart. A hardwood pole 6 ft. long supports the feeder.

one feeder out of sight of each other. Hummingbirds are very territorial and a single bird may try to dominate one feeder, so it's always a good idea to have a place for other hummingbirds to feed.

The wonderful thing about bird feeders—aside from the many feathered friends they attract—is that they can add a decorative element to any yard or garden. If you prefer to buy a feeder, you will find a vast selection of design styles, from cement or stone statuary molded with large dishes for holding seed to quaint hanging gazebos with windows showing the seeds inside; from rustic, loglike tube feeders to eye-catching blown-glass hummingbird feeders. You can even purchase novelty feeders to add a bit of fun to the yard. Of course, you may prefer to make your own, in which case the design is limited only by your imagination. Birds are not design critics; they are looking for nutritious food and a safe place to eat it. Beyond that, the look of the feeder should satisfy you. But be aware that the more conspicuous the feeder is, the more obvious it will be to predators.

If you decide to take the hands-on approach, it is best to use natural materials. Wood is the preferred building material, but you should never use wood that has been treated in any way. You can also use plastic or other materials as long as they are nontoxic and don't tend to overheat (like uninsulated metal, usually a bad choice for birdhouses).

ADVICE FROM A BIRDER Certain birds, most notably blue jays, will go to great lengths to ensure they have good sources of calcium. Unfortunately, this can mean that the birds will actually chip paint off a house in a search of the mineral. If this happens in your yard, supply an alternate source of calcium, such as crushed eggshells, and you'll save the finish on your house!

FEEDER FOOD

As far as the birds are concerned, what you put inside the feeder is much more important than what the feeder itself looks like. You can certainly buy birdseed mixes to fill feeders, and birds will gladly eat it. But at certain times of the year, such as fall and winter, it's important that birds get as much protein, calories and fats in the form of oils as possible. That's why at those times—and other times if you can afford it—a better choice is a more select seed mix or individual seed type.

Black sunflower seeds are excellent oil-rich seeds, with a soft covering that birds find easy to tear through.

PAN NAILED TO TREE TRUNK MAKES GOOD BIRD FEEDER

Desiring an inexpensive bird feeder of large capacity, one farmer nailed a pan to a tree and then soldered 1/2-in. wire mesh over the lower half as indicated, leaving the upper portion open so that the food supply could be replenished. The feeder was kept filled with wheat heads. After picking the wheat grains from the heads, the birds pulled the empty ones through the wire and dropped them so that they could get at the filled heads.

FEEDING TRAY FOR BIRDS

A western businessman and nature lover installed feeding trays at several points around his thickly shrubbed and forested yard so that his bird guests could eat removed from the danger of cats, dogs and other molesters. He set lengths of pipe into the ground, and the galvanized-iron feeding trays were fitted to rods sliding into these pipes. When a tray has to be filled it is lowered, and then it is raised so that the birds may eat in safety. To raise the tray, the rod is slid upward and a pin is inserted through a hole in the pipe, underneath the lower end of the rod.

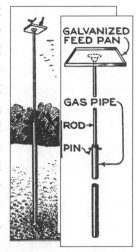

GALVANIZED FEED PAN

GAS PIPE

ROD

PIN

Striped sunflower seed, although not as rich and easy to eat as black sunflower seed, is a good choice for larger birds with tougher beaks, such as jays, woodpeckers, grosbeaks and cardinals. Some stores sell shelled sunflower seeds that take the work out of it for the birds and eliminate much of the mess that often accumulates under feeders. They may also offer custom blends, incorporating pieces of fruit with a variety of seeds. These are usually meant to attract certain types of birds, such

SIMPLE HUMMINGBIRD FEEDER

A hummingbird feeder adds an interesting touch to a lawn or garden and is easy and inexpensive to make. The first require-ment is an empty plastic medicine bottle or vial with a watertight cover. The bot-tom of the bottle is drilled so that a $1/4$-in. plastic or glass tube, about $2^1/2$ in. long, will fit snugly. The tube should be bent slightly as illustrated. Any one of the plastic-metal compounds or plastic cements may be used to secure the tube in position.

The same adhesive is used to fasten a short piece of chain to the top of the cover. After the cement has dried, fill the bottle with a mixture of water sweetened with sugar or honey. Suspend the feeder from a tree or post.

as songbirds. One caveat: If you opt for a less expensive seed mix, keep an eye on the ground under the feeder. Birds can be particular about the seeds they eat, and they may end up rejecting half the filler in a seed mix, strewing rejected food all over the ground in their search for the good stuff. This may ultimately make a cheaper seed mix much more costly in the long run.

Safflower seeds are another alternative favored by many backyard birds. White millet is an inexpensive alternative that appeals to juncos and mourning doves. But if you're not all that worried about expense and you want to offer the birds in your yard a gourmet treat, you should consider niger. Niger (sometimes sold as nyjer) is a jet-black oilseed that is a favorite of many common backyard birds including purple finches, goldfinches, pine siskins and redpolls. Niger is extremely nutritious, offering birds abundant quality calories and a high oil content. Niger feeders are specially designed to limit or prevent spillage because it is very expensive—the one downside to this seed.

Not all birds, however, are seed enthusiasts. If you want to cater to different tastes, consider putting out mealworms or other bagged insect mixes for birds such as jays, bluebirds, titmice, wrens and robins. If you prefer to give your hummingbirds something better than a mix of sugar and water, you'll find a range of high-energy nectars available from the sources you use for your seed. In general, bird food of all kinds can be found at well-equipped feed stores, nurseries and home centers.

One of the most popular bird foods is suet. Suet is a mixture of animal fat, seeds and filler and is considered a delicacy by an incredible diversity of bird species. Although you can buy suet cakes at any time of the year, they are most useful around breeding time because they offer fat-rich sources of nutrients, and in the winter, when they provide great nutritional benefit in a compact food source. It is sometimes put out in summer, but in extreme heat suet may go rancid and spoil. Suet is generally purchased in cakes that balance a mix of rendered fats, seeds and other additives. Although you can make your own at home, you may find it a challenge because the mixture of components and types of fat have to be correct to entice birds. Suet is generally placed in hanging wire cages or other feeders that allow access while providing a holder for the slippery cakes.

LOCATION, LOCATION, LOCATION

If you go to the trouble of buying a feeder, filling it with good food and tending to it over the course of the season, you will certainly want to be able to watch the birds that show up for a free meal. But locating the feeder based solely on its visibility from a window or the back porch may not be ideal. You need to carefully consider the location of your feeders to ensure that you don't put your backyard birds in jeopardy while you're trying to help them fill up.

The best feeder location is the safest location. Hanging feeders should be placed away from any structure that might let potential predators get at the birds while they eat. For instance, hanging a feeder over a shrub is a probably a bad idea, as is

BIRD FEEDER FROM MIXING BOWLS

Here is a simple bird feeder that anyone can make. It consists of two wooden mixing bowls, one about 2 in. larger than the other, and a length of large dowel. Three drain holes are drilled in the smaller bowl, after which both bowls are attached to the ends of the dowel with screw eyes as shown. The feeder can be suspended between two tree branches.

placing it right under an eave on a roof easily accessible to squirrels or cats.

The best location for a feeder offers the birds a clear view in all directions so that they can easily see any threat coming long before it arrives. That means keeping a clear circle without tall ornamental grasses or shrubs about 10 ft. in diameter around the feeder. Keep this in mind before you decide to landscape around a feeding platform on a pole. Whenever you place a feeder, consider how a predator might reach it. If you hang a tubular feeder from a branch, is the branch strong enough to support a cat or squirrel? If so, move it to a more delicate branch.

TENDING FEEDERS

B ird feeders require a certain amount of maintenance to keep the birds coming back. First and foremost, you need to keep them filled. Birds are creatures of habit. If they know a certain location—such as one of your feeders—is a reliable food source, birds will make a point of coming to the feeder on a regular basis.

QUICKIE CLOTHESLINE BIRD FEEDER

A quick and effective bird feeder can be hung out away from trees to keep it safe from cats. It's just a cardboard box cover slipped through wire coat hangers. Bend the

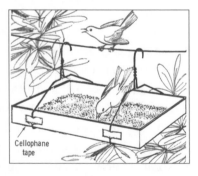

Cellophane tape

hangers as necessary and tape the cover to them.

BIRD FEEDERS FROM GOURDS

Certain types of ornamental gourds provide natural, attractive and efficient bird feeders. For example, a gourd shaped similar to the one shown can be converted into a feeder by cutting a slot in the upper surface of the curved end and inserting two dowels for perches. It is filled through a small hole in the upper end;

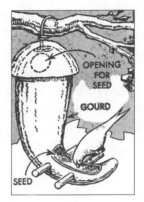

the hole is covered by a cap cut from the end of a larger gourd. The length of the feeding slot will depend on the exact shape at the point where it is made. The slot should be of a length and shape that keeps the feed from spilling, yet permits the birds to peck at it.

However, if the supply is spotty and irregular, they are going to search for more consistent food source.

But feeders also need to be cleaned and fixed from time to time. Just how often depends on how many birds the feeder services and where you live. In areas with high humidity, bird food can go bad very quickly, so you may need to change it on occasion. You also need to clean the feeders to avoid fungus or other possible contaminants. Wash them with a strong detergent solution, rinsing them well and letting them dry completely

LADDER HOIST SWINGS
HEAVY BIRDHOUSE ON POLE

If you have occasion to put up or take down a large birdhouse or do other light hoisting jobs, this simple hoist and a ladder will enable you to do the work easily. As shown, the hoist is supported on a rung of the ladder, where it is held by turn buttons and two cleats nailed to the underside of the horizontal support piece.

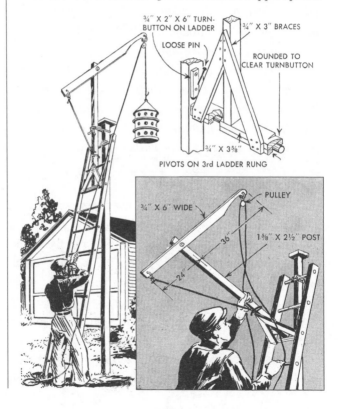

¾" X 2" X 6" TURN-BUTTON ON LADDER

¾" X 3" BRACES

LOOSE PIN

ROUNDED TO CLEAR TURNBUTTON

¾" X 3⅝"

PIVOTS ON 3rd LADDER RUNG

PULLEY

¾" X 6" WIDE

36"

24"

1⅝" X 2½" POST

> *A cross-arm is held at the desired angle by a rope tied to the upright, while the upright is tied to the bird-house pole. The ladder itself is also tied to the pole. After the house has been raised to the necessary height, the hoisting rope is tied to the ladder; the rope, which secures the hoist, is let out until the hoist swings back far enough to ease the house into position.*

before putting them back in service. Because fewer birds feed at night, nighttime is a good time for cleaning feeders. Most bird enthusiasts clean their feeders once or twice a month, but you should inspect the feeders and clean them whenever they are dirty. Nobody likes to eat in filth, including birds.

You should also inspect your feeders for structural integrity on a regular basis. Fix cracks in the feeder body or any damage to the hanging or support structures: You don't want a feeder falling while birds are eating.

INVITING HUNGRY BIRDS TO THE GARDEN

Your garden itself can be a lush kitchen for feathered visitors. Attracting birds to feed in (and on) your landscape is first and foremost a question of diversity. The greater the mix of plants you use, the greater the potential bounty for any avian visitor. A diversity of plants also invites a variety of insects in the yard, further expanding a bird's potential menu options and making the yard attractive to more species.

Consequently, if you want the largest number of bird visitors possible, include a pleasing mix of trees, shrubs and flowering annuals and perennials in your yard. Whenever possible, choose plants with different bloom seasons to stagger and prolong the food supply for the birds in the garden. And keep in mind what species you would most like to invite into your yard when selecting your plants and designing your landscape. If you have favorites, choose plants those species prefer.

ORGANIC MEANS SAFE

Pesticides can be fatal to all small winged creatures. The smallest of all—such as hummingbirds—are especially at risk. If you really want to make your garden bird-friendly, choose organic or natural pest solutions when planting flowers and shrubs. Or, better yet, let the pests come—they are just another attraction to the birds you want to watch.

For instance, the enchanting and ever-busy hummingbirds will frequent a landscape rich in nectar plants, including honeysuckle, trumpet vine and magnolia. If these are problematic plants to grow in your zone, understand that hummingbirds are generally attracted to red and yellow tubular flowers. They also feed on small flying insects attracted by these types of flowers. Colder-zone plants known to attract hummingbirds—and other nectar-loving birds for that matter—include cardinal flowers, scarlet salvia, bee balm and pink or red penstemons.

If you enjoy songbirds—and who doesn't?—supply sources of seeds for these seed-loving species. Ornamental grasses with large seed heads, sunflowers and, in the west, oriental poppies are good seed sources for sparrows, catbirds, tanagers, nuthatches and other songbirds. Yarrow seeds are a favorite of ground feeders such as the mourning dove. Other birds that enjoy seeds in their diets include finches and buntings. Flowers that

BIRDS PREVENTED FROM DISTURBING
NEW GRAFTS WITH LONG PERCHES

After grafting, a gardener often lost valuable scions because birds would alight on them and displace them. Noticing that the birds always alighted on the highest scion, he prevented the trouble by providing perches that extended a few inches above the scions. The perches are merely small sticks taped or tied to the parent branch. One perch will protect two or more scions if the latter are on the same branch. When the grafts become strong enough to support a bird, the perches should be removed.

provide a good long season of blooming and plentiful seeds include coreopsis, black-eyed Susans, asters and purple coneflowers. If you're in the habit of deadheading (removing spent blooms from the plant), consider leaving one or two blooms to dry up completely on the stalk. The birds in your yard will thank you for it.

Another type of feeder that has recently gained in popularity is the fruit feeder. Many species of birds feed on fruit, and fruit feeders are an easy way to draw these species into the yard with the small expense of a few pieces of apple or other fruit. The beautiful nectar-eating oriole loves to fill up on orange halves, and you'll find feeders in stores built just to hold oranges. Cardinals, robins and many other birds also enjoy a little citrus or apples—just cut them or otherwise remove the skin so that the birds can easily get at the flesh. And you don't have to limit yourself (or the birds) to oranges and apples: Cardinals are particularly enamored of pomegranate seeds.

If you're willing to sacrifice a little bit of your crop, you may be surprised at the sensational bird-watching opportunities you'll enjoy in return. For instance, the beautiful blue jay will eat cherries whole off the tree, as will the woodpecker. Finches, thrashers and quail have a sweet tooth for currants and gooseberries, making those shrubs excellent foundation plantings for bird-loving homes. Anything small enough to be carried away or eaten whole is very attractive to birds.

It's the rare bird that doesn't enjoy raiding a plot of wild or domestic strawberry plants, and the same is true of blackberry and raspberry brambles. But birds of all kinds especially love smaller, easy-to-pick berries.

BIRDS UNABLE TO DAMAGE CORN WITH EARS TIED AT TOP

You can protect your sweet corn from birds that peck at its ends by tying the tops of the husks with thread or cord when the kernels start to develop. The birds, unable to tear the ear open from the side, will no longer be able to reach the kernels.

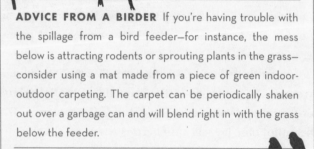

This makes the beautyberry an ideal shrub for many gardens. The lavender berries attract a range of birds, including the mockingbird, and the flowers provide an additional benefit for attracting colorful butterflies (and, therefore, birds that prefer a live meal). The lantana is another favorite of berry-loving birds. Shrubs and trees that grow berries inedible to humans are sometimes the best choices because you won't be competing with your feathered visitors for a share of the crop.

KEEPING SOME
FOR YOURSELF

If you've done a good job planting a landscape that attracts a variety of birds (a process some experts call birdscaping), you'll have plenty of subjects dropping by for a meal. The problem is, birds don't differentiate between the pyracantha berries that you intended for them and the blueberries you hoped to keep for yourself. Your success in bringing birds to the garden might just turn into failure to bring your favorite fruits to the kitchen table.

That's why you may want to protect your treasured fruit and vegetable plants from the appetites of local flying feeders. Birds have a lousy sense of smell, so any kind of odor-based deterrent isn't going to work. The scarecrow principle is only slightly more effective. While you can find a range of fake predator birds at garden shops and home centers, these usually only work for a while (even a bird gets wise to the fact that something that never moves is not a threat) and only with certain species. Some people have a bit more success with

---

PROTECT PLANTS FROM BIRDS

Enjoy birds in your backyard without having to get rid of your garden. Protect seedlings and strawberry plants from thieves with a portable garden frame made from a pair of modified coat hangers and two panes of glass. A batten with holes drilled through it slips over hangers to brace them and hold the glass in place.

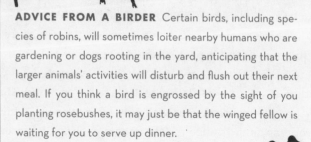

ADVICE FROM A BIRDER Certain birds, including species of robins, will sometimes loiter nearby humans who are gardening or dogs rooting in the yard, anticipating that the larger animals' activities will disturb and flush out their next meal. If you think a bird is engrossed by the sight of you planting rosebushes, it may just be that the winged fellow is waiting for you to serve up dinner.

hanging shiny objects from fruit tree branches. Pie tins or aluminum foil sculptures sometimes do the job, and anything that clangs is even better. But you wind up making the garden look less attractive and, again, birds get wise. Netting is one of the most effective solutions because used correctly, it physically prevents the birds from getting to the fruit.

Ultimately, luring a diversity of birds to your yard may just mean sacrificing a portion of your crop to the hungry hordes. In exchange, you get the company and viewing pleasure of some of the most intriguing members of the animal kingdom, a trade-off many people feel is well worth it.

CHAPTER 4

HOME SWEET HOME

There's no better way to ensure excellent bird-watching opportunities than to give birds a place to live. Not every bird will agree to dorm in a man-made home, but the ones who do will reward your generosity with an intimate glimpse into their lives that you'll rarely see anywhere else.

ADVICE FROM A BIRDER Although the best time to inaugurate a birdhouse is right before nesting season, this doesn't mean you can't put up the one you've just built in the middle of winter. Even if birds don't use the house to nest right away, it can serve as a safe haven for birds in transit or those that just need temporary protection from inclement weather.

WHICH HOUSE IS BEST

A s with feeders, no single birdhouse is right for all the visitors to your yard. Each bird has its own nesting requirements, and any birdhouse you install will be suitable for a modest number of species. The differences lie largely in the birdhouse's dimensions, the most important being that of the entrance hole, which will determine what types of birds can get in—and which will be kept out (along with potential predators).

For instance, a birdhouse meant for goldfinches should be built with an entrance hole 1½ in. in diameter, preferably protected with a predator guard. Wrens and swallows require a smaller entrance hole, usually 1¼ in. in diameter—except for English swallows, which are a

---

SPRINGY PORCH ON WREN HOUSE

Though most birds are too large to enter the opening to a wren house—which needs no perch—they do sometimes attempt to enter and may annoy the wrens. To discourage this, one man provided a perch consisting of a short dowel on the end of a short spring wire. Heavier intruders were frightened away when trying to alight on it because the perch was not strong enough to support them.

WREN HOUSE

SPRING WIRE

TRICK PERCH

ADVICE FROM A BIRDER You may be tempted to place different birdhouses for multiple families near each other so to facilitate viewing opportunities. Unfortunately, you may find that only one of the houses becomes occupied. Because birds are territorial, the first inhabitant in the area may drive away potential occupants of the other houses. The same is true for birdbaths and feeders that are positioned near birdhouses. To invite the greatest number of birds into your yard, keep birdhouses far away from other birdhouses and bird-friendly yard features.

bit bigger and an aggressive species that will attempt to bully other birds out of a birdhouse.

Regardless of the type of bird you're trying to accommodate with the birdhouse you make or hang, a predator guard is a good idea. These range from a baffle placed over the entrance hole to an entrance tunnel created by a long piece of pipe mounted with a flange on the front of the hole. The goal is the same—to prevent larger, more aggressive species from taking over the nest, and to stop marauders such as squirrels, raccoons and cats from reaching in and destroying eggs or attacking the nesting birds.

If you have questions about the actual dimensions of a house you want to make for birds in your backyard, you can find plans for species-specific birdhouses at some craft stores and larger pet stores; you can also find an amazing variety online. The plans are usually very basic and allow for customization so you can make the birdhouse suit your garden and your tastes.

You can also opt to buy a house. Just make sure the house you buy will serve the birds you are hoping to house and watch.

SIX UNUSUAL WREN HOUSES

All the wren houses illustrated here were prizewinners and have proved their worth by being occupied during the entire season. One of the simplest homes for a wren can be made from a coconut shell. The top is cut off and holes are drilled for three wires. These are twisted together and slipped through a hole in the top,

and a 7/8-in. hole is cut in the side. The shell may be painted or left plain, as you desire, and hung up on one of the lower branches of a tree.

On the top of page 101 is a picture of a birdhouse built to resemble a Dutch windmill. This one is particularly adapted for use on a shelf, for hanging from the edge of the roof or for mounting on a pole in your garden. The details of making this type are given in the lower illustration; 1/4-in. stock is used. A small gallery

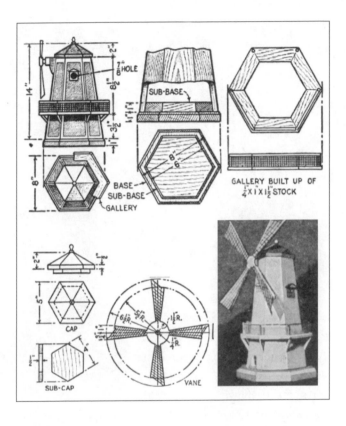

is fitted around the walls, 3½ in. from the base. Small split dowels are set at each corner to support the railing, which is a 1-in. width of wire mesh with a narrow band of tin crimped around its top to form the upper rail. The base consists of two pieces, one extending beyond the edges of the house and the other tapered to fit inside the nesting space. A hinge and hook-and-eye hold the base, which is removable for the purpose of cleaning.

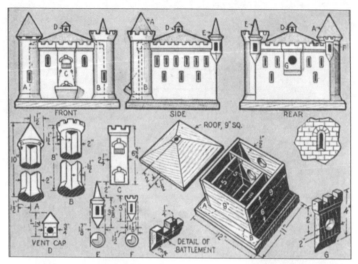

Another pleasing type is one made to represent a castle. It is essentially a box, 8 in. square, with the bottom projecting beyond the sides. The interior is separated by partitions as shown, which provide

insulating air spaces around the nesting place. The roof is made from a block, and the towers are turned to shape and then grooved to fit the corners of the box. A drawbridge may be made from stripping grooved wood to simulate the side rails and fastened to the entrance by means of small screw eyes and chains. The actual doorway is cut through a small tower rising at the center of the back.

Also shown is an acorn house, which is suspended from a tree branch or the eaves of a building by means

HANGING A WREN HOUSE

An easy way to suspend a wren house from a tree limb is to use a wire coat hanger. Cut the hanger at the cross at one end and bend the opposite wire to form a loop. Insert the crossbar through holes in the peak of the house, then through the loop, and secure.

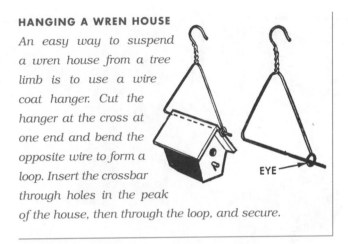

EYE

of a screw eye through the top. If a lathe is available, the project can be turned and the nesting place forced out. The inside of the cap is grooved to take dowels, which hold the body and cap together.

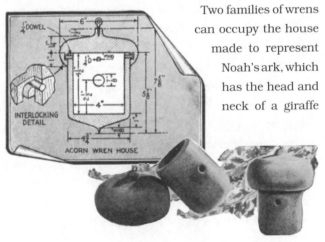

Two families of wrens can occupy the house made to represent Noah's ark, which has the head and neck of a giraffe

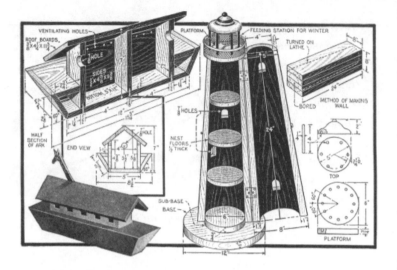

projecting above the roof. The bottom is screwed to the sides so that it can be removed for cleaning the interior. A grotesque effect may be created by cutting out animal heads and placing them so they appear to be peering over the sides. Don't add too many of them, though, and make sure they are dull in color, without sharp points or shiny spots, or the birds will not use the house.

The lighthouse, detailed above right, differs from the other houses in that it contains four nesting spaces with staggered doorways. A winter feeding station is provided at the top and resembles the lamp of a lighthouse. It can be turned and bored out on a lathe by first gluing four pieces of 2 x 8-in. stock together. Or it can be made with hand tools by gluing two pieces together separately and gouging out their centers, then hinging them together as shown. In either case, the house should be made in two sections to facilitate cleaning. All birdhouses should be provided with substantial supports and put up early in the fall, well ahead of the arrival of the songsters.

INSULATED WREN HOUSES OF METAL

You can make attractive wren houses that will be cool and comfortable inside using empty tin cans, scrap wood and corrugated cardboard. Those pictured in *Figures 1* and *4* (on pages 106 and 108) are examples of what can be done with round 1-gal. cans. In *Figure 1*, the can is used in a vertical position and a wooden base is substituted for the can bottom, which is removed. In the circular detail, note the unique locking feature used to hold the base for easy removal when cleaning the house. The top and sides are insulated with three layers of corrugated cardboard, and the sides are vented for air circulation. One long bolt attaches the roof, which is also insulated. A linoleum overlay around the entrance adds a decorative touch. In *Figure 4*, a can is used in a horizontal position. Both ends are removed and replaced with jigsawed wooden ends. Circular cleats or rings are screwed to the wooden ends and slip into the can, which is nailed to the cleats. An opening for cleaning, covered with a compression-type can lid, is screwed into place.

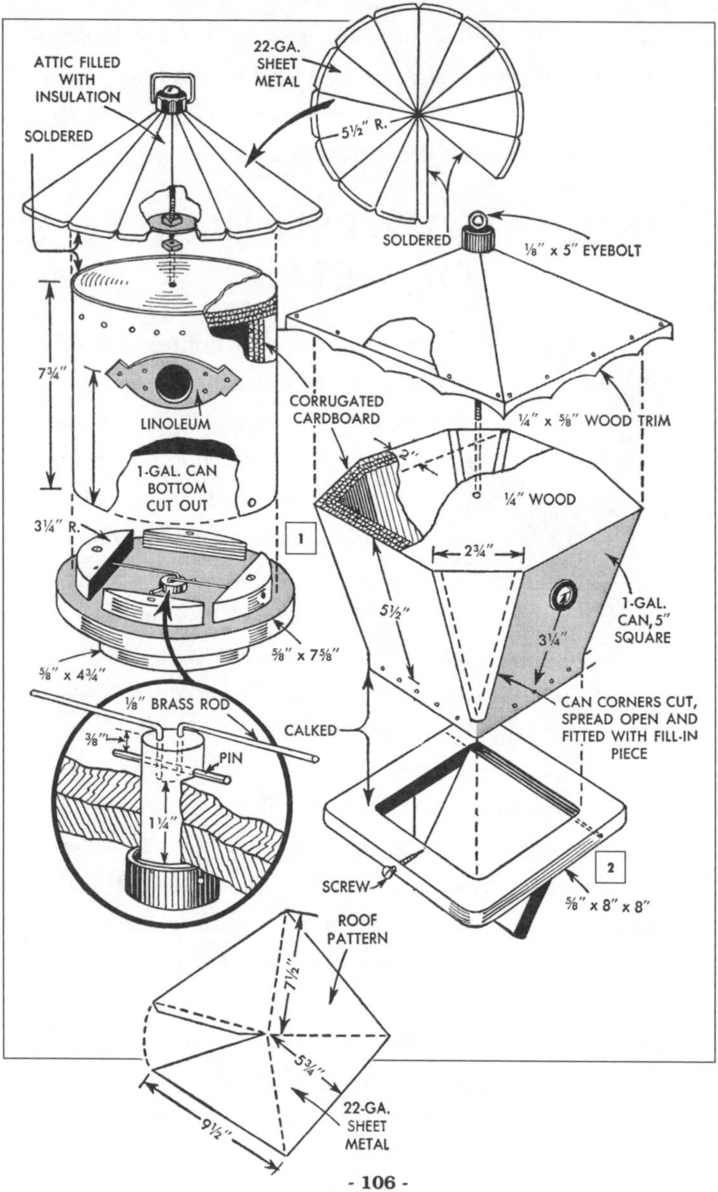
ATTIC FILLED WITH INSULATION
SOLDERED
22-GA. SHEET METAL
5½" R.
SOLDERED
⅛" x 5" EYEBOLT
7¾"
LINOLEUM
1-GAL. CAN BOTTOM CUT OUT
CORRUGATED CARDBOARD
¼" x ⅝" WOOD TRIM
2"
¼" WOOD
3¼" R.
1
2¾"
5½"
1-GAL. CAN, 5" SQUARE
3¼"
⅝" x 7⅝"
⅝" x 4¾"
⅛" BRASS ROD
⅜"
PIN
1¼"
CALKED
CAN CORNERS CUT, SPREAD OPEN AND FITTED WITH FILL-IN PIECE
SCREW
2
⅝" x 8" x 8"
ROOF PATTERN
7½"
5¾"
9½"
22-GA. SHEET METAL

How old tin cans and scrap wood can be utilized in building durable wren houses that stay cool inside. Each design has a handy arrangement for cleaning out old nests

Three layers of cardboard inside the can insulate the house, which is roofed with 1/4-in. wood. To add a decorative touch, nail strips of perforated metal screen to the roof edges. When assembling the ends to the can, be sure that they allow at least 1/8-in. clearance between the can and the roof. This is to permit air to pass under the eaves and out of vent holes in the gable ends to cool the attic.

The houses in *Figures 2* and *3* are assembled from square cans. In *Figure 2*, both ends of the can are removed and a wooden top and base are used. Notice that the center portion of the base is pivoted for easy cleaning. A long screw through one edge of the base locks the pivoted portion in the closed position. To obtain the can's unusual shape, slit the corners and solder triangular fill-in pieces to them after spreading the top of the can. Scrolled wood decorates the edges of the metal roof, which is attached by a long eyebolt. Further decoration is added by placing a plastic or linoleum ring around the entrance hole.

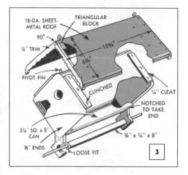

The end containing the entrance opening of the house in *Figure 3* swings outward for cleaning. It is held by a pivot pin at the top and by two screws at the bottom. Cleats are nailed to the can near the ends

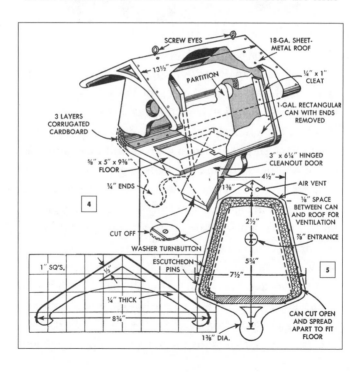

for attaching the roof, the latter being reinforced at the ridge by triangular corner blocks to take screw eyes; these are for suspending the house.

The neat shape of the house in *Figure 5* is obtained by using a rectangular can opened at one side, which is spread and nailed to the wooden floor of the house. A clean-out door, closed by a turn button fashioned from a washer, is provided in the floor. The roof is metal with jigsawed trim at the ends. Cardboard insulation is used inside the can, and holes are provided in the wooden ends to ventilate the attic.

ADVICE FROM A BIRDER Sometimes, the backyard birder experiences the frustration of having a birdhouse go unused. If this happens, change the location the following year, and try to make the house even more attractive by adding sanitary cotton batting or balls, or fresh sawdust, all of which will make the home more appealing. You can also try changing the types of food you supply, which in turn may attract different species more inclined to use the lodgings provided.

BIRDHOUSE MADE OF AN OLD STRAW HAT

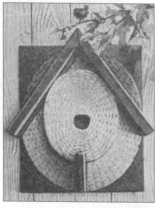

A birdhouse made of an old straw hat is a practical and easily contrived affair. Cut a hole in the crown of the hat, then nail the hat against a board of proper size. To protect the hat against the rain, put a roof over it as shown. A perch is also provided. Such a birdhouse can be hung against the trunk of a tree or nailed against a wall. Leaving the hat in its natural straw color and painting the rest dark brown produces a satisfying effect.

ROUGH, RUGGED AND RUSTIC BIRDHOUSES

B irds are more likely to occupy houses if the nesting cavities are adapted to their requirements. A chart of inside dimensions for houses is provided. After deciding which species of birds you wish to attract, make the houses to suit them. The hanging log house in *Figure 1* is an attractive ornament even when birds are not in residence. To make it, split a seasoned log with a handsaw, chisel out the inside to the dimensions given and bore the proper size entrance hole. Then bolt the log together at the ends so that it can be taken apart for cleaning.

Robins and barn swallows require a fairly large house with one open side, as in *Figure 2*. This is easy to make if firewood slabs are available. Thin bark is used for the purple martin house in *Figure 3*. The bark is wrapped halfway around two end disks, bound with green willow, split and then secured

CHICKADEE, NUTHATCH, TITMOUSE DOWNY WOODPECKER

RAFFIA OR DRY GRASS, ALL SEEDS REMOVED

1¼" OR 1⅛" HOLE

9"

1

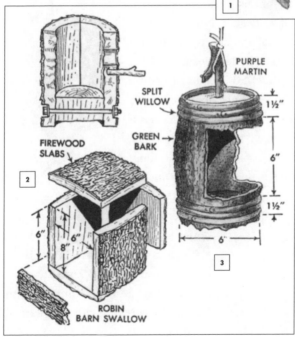

FIREWOOD SLABS

SPLIT WILLOW

GREEN BARK

PURPLE MARTIN

1½"

6"

1½"

6"

6"

6"

8"

ROBIN BARN SWALLOW

2

3

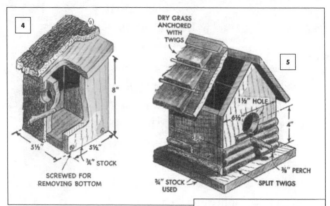

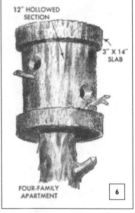

12" HOLLOWED SECTION

3" X 14" SLAB

FOUR-FAMILY APARTMENT

with brads. *Figure 4* shows a simple design built of 3/4-in. material and covered with bark taken from dead logs.

Bluebirds will like the little thatched-roof cabin shown in *Figure 5.* The walls are covered with split twigs, and straw or grass is used for the thatching, which is held down with anchor poles. If you can find a hol-

low log, most of the work on the four-family apartment house in *Figure 6* is done, except for the slabs on top and bottom. Bore holes of the required size and install partitions and perches. If a log has only a small hole in the center, it can be enlarged by burning it out.

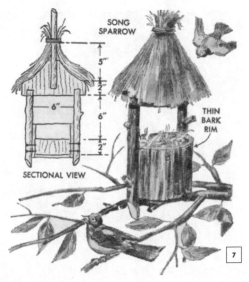

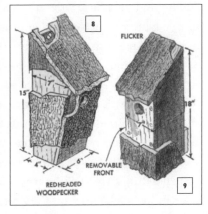

The song sparrow isn't as exclusive as most birds and likes a house with all sides open, like the miniature summer house in *Figure 7*. It can be set on the end of a tree branch, provided it is not over 3 ft. aboveground.

On the other hand, the flicker and red-headed woodpecker demand privacy and considerable depth. Homes for them are illustrated in *Figures 8* and *9*. They are merely wooden boxes covered with bark and attached

to a tree trunk. The fronts should be screwed in place for easy removal when cleaning time comes around. The little cottage in *Figure 10* will interest the phoebe if the front wall is left out, and the house wren if it is left in. Use material surfaced on one side only, rough side out, and shingle with strips of thin bark.

To attract birds, scatter the kind of food they like. The kinds of fruit and berry bushes around your home will determine the species of birds that will congregate there. Those that remain through the winter like suet. A suet stick fitted with perches (as in *Figure 11*) and suspended in a tree will be well patronized. Bore 1-in. holes in the stick and stuff the holes with the suet.

BIRD HOUSES MADE FROM HELMETS

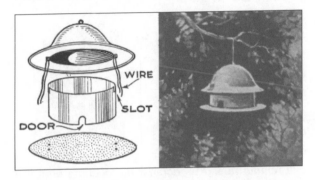

A novel use for retired trench helmets is shown in the photograph and drawing. The strap and cushion are removed from the helmet. A wire loop or ring is placed through the hole in the center of the crown. The base is cut from a piece of galvanized iron upon which the outline of the helmet has been traced. A 5-in. length of 8-in. furnace pipe is placed in the helmet, and slots are cut in opposite sides to allow it to pass the metal strap loops. Next, the arched door is cut on the lower edge of the piping. If intended as a wren house, a hole the size of a quarter is large enough. Two 15-in. pieces of wire are placed through the strap loops and bent at the center. Four holes, two on each side, are punched through the base and the ends of the wire are inserted, then brought together and twisted or tied as neatly as possible. Birdhouses should be built in the winter or early spring so that when birds are ready to nest, there will be no odor of paint remaining.

If you want to keep sparrows out of a martin house between the time the martins leave in the fall and return in the spring, substitute a pivoted shelf for the regular perch, as indicated. Then the perch will remain tipped up against the opening until it is time for the birds to return in spring.

COOL BIRDHOUSES OF CEMENT

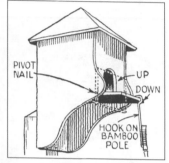

Everyone who has built houses to attract birds has probably wanted to make round and odd-shaped houses with irregular roofs, either for the novelty of their appearance or to blend in with the surroundings. This pleasure is often foregone because of the difficulty of shaping such houses from wood (metal being out of the question because the houses would become too hot). But you can get any shape you desire with a material consisting of 1 part portland cement and 3 parts regular premixed cement.

This material dries slowly so that you have plenty of time to mold it as desired. If kept out of the sun and wind so that it dries as slowly as possible, it will become very hard. It can be troweled smooth or left rough, and will take paint nicely, making it possible to

build houses finished in bright colors to help dress up the garden.

To use this plasterlike material, all you need is a framework to which to apply it. The martin house in *Figures 1* and *2* is a good example. The ends are solid wood

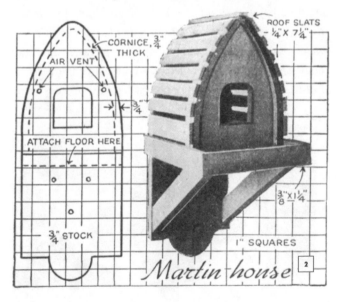

Martin house

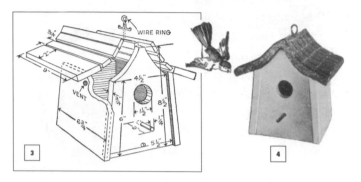

and the roof, which is covered with the material, is made of slats. Robins usually build on a shelf of some kind but will not nest in a closed house. The shelter in *Figure 3* is attractive to them. Only the roof is covered with the cement mix, which is molded to resemble bark. A few small nails projecting from the roof slats help to anchor the mixture. The bluebird house in *Figure 4* is of solid wood, but the roof is covered with the cement mix and molded to simulate shingles. A woodpecker is one bird that insists on building in a hollow log, but it is easier to

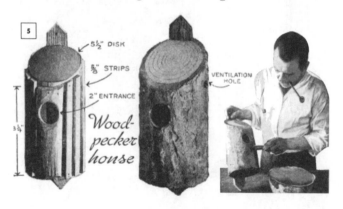

make the "log" shown in *Figure 5* than it is to find a real one that is hollow. Assemble the skeleton framework and cover the outside roughly with the cement mix, allowing it to dry for a day or so. Then apply a second coat, reproducing as nearly as possible the bark of the tree.

Now comes a home for the little house wren. The one shown in *Figure 6* is easy to make and is entirely covered with the cement mix. The framework consists of slats nailed to wood disks at the top and bottom. Also, the roof is made

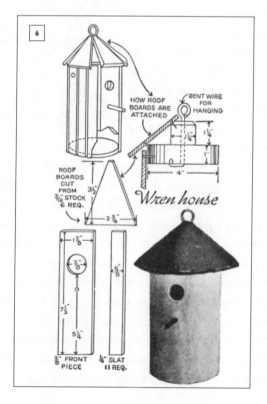

of slats, which are shaped and assembled as in the upper detail. Be sure to make the entrance opening small enough to keep out other birds, or the wren will vacate its home. The house can be hung in the branches of a thickly foliaged tree or under the cornice of a building.

DETACHABLE BIRDHOUSES

It is becoming quite the fashion for country, suburb and even city dwellers to provide small birdhouses in yards and parks. They are usually mounted on poles or in trees. Because they are securely fastened, it is not an easy matter to remove them when they need to be repainted, repaired or cleaned, as is occasionally necessary. A method of mounting a birdhouse so that it can readily be detached is shown in the drawing. The top of the supporting post is trimmed down to fit loosely inside a No. 2 fruit can, which is cut and slotted as shown. The can is nailed to the underside of the birdhouse and slipped over the end of the pole. Nails are then driven into the slots and bent downward at right angles as shown, so that the can will not slip off. When removing the birdhouse, the nails are turned to the position shown in the lower detail; the house can then be easily released with an upward pull.

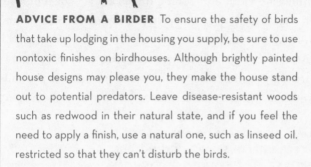

MODEL YOUR HOME
FOR THE BIRDS

B y simplifying the details of construction, almost any style of house can be modeled to make an attractive home for birds. The details and dimensions given are for a scale model of one particu-lar style, but much of the general construction can be followed to make any model. Only two dormers are shown, *Figures 1* and *2*, with openings to the second floor. If desired, two more compartments can be added at the back by building a single dormer of sufficient width and adding the floors as shown in front in *Figure 1*. Use ¼-in. plywood for the second floors. Use ½-in. waterproof plywood for all the parts of the exterior except the dormers and roof; use ¼-in. waterproof plywood for the latter. Fasten the sides to the ends with screws in countersunk holes, which you can plug

MAKE THE PARTS FOR THE DORMERS AND THE
PORCH ENTRY OF SCRAP STOCK, AND CUT
THEM A TRIFLE OVERSIZE SO THAT YOU CAN
PLANE THEM TO FIT AFTER ASSEMBLY.

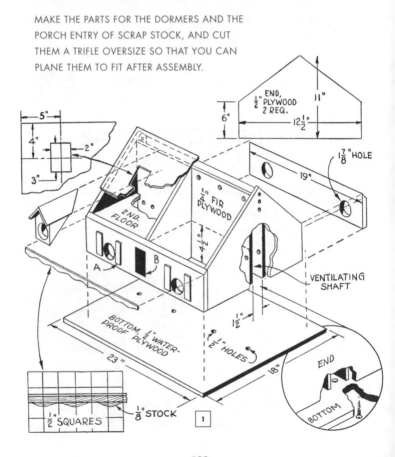

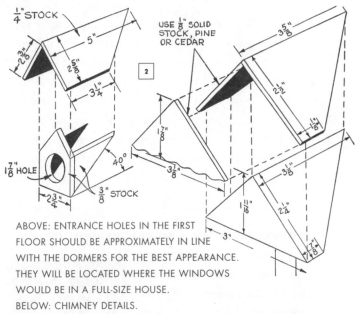

ABOVE: ENTRANCE HOLES IN THE FIRST
FLOOR SHOULD BE APPROXIMATELY IN LINE
WITH THE DORMERS FOR THE BEST APPEARANCE.
THEY WILL BE LOCATED WHERE THE WINDOWS
WOULD BE IN A FULL-SIZE HOUSE.
BELOW: CHIMNEY DETAILS.

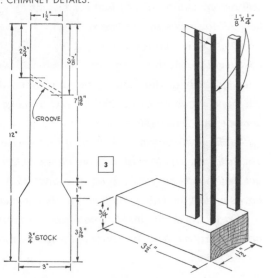

- 123 -

with dowels. Then fit the ventilating shaft and bore ³/8-in. holes for the passage of air, as in *Figure 1*. For purple martins the entrance holes should be at least 1⁷/8 in. in diameter. The shutters, *A*, are made by ripping ¹/8-in. strips from ³/4-in. stock and cutting off 4-in. lengths. These are nailed in place with brads after painting the front of the house. The front door, *B*, is simply represented by painting a rectangular area black. *Figure 3* details the chimney, fitted after the house is assembled.

PROPER DESIGN FOR A MARTIN BIRDHOUSE

This birdhouse was designed and built to make a home for the American martin. The house will accommodate twenty families. All the holes are arranged so they will not be open to the cold winds from the north that often kill the birds that come in the early spring. Around each opening is an extra ring of wood to make a longer passage that assists the martin inside in fighting off the English sparrow, which may try to drive it out. The holes are made oval to allow all the little ones to get their heads out for fresh air. The long, overhanging eaves protect the little birds from the hot summer sun.

Partitions on the inside create rooms so that each opening has a room. The inside of the rooms should be stained black.

A PIGEON HOUSE

Pigeon houses need not be eyesores, as is often the case. They can, in fact, be made to harmonize with their surroundings, adding beauty to a dull spot and even making the grounds around your home more attractive. The house described will accommodate twenty pigeons, and additional stories of the same type may be built on to provide for more. Nearly all of the wood necessary may be obtained from boxes, and the other materials are also readily available at minimal cost. The construction is such that a boy or girl handy with ordinary carpentry tools can undertake it successfully.

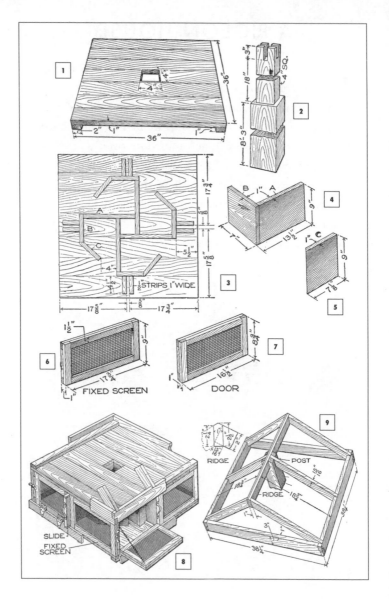

1

2

4″ SQ.
4″×3″
18″
8′-3″

3

A
B
C
17¾″
⁵⁄₈″
5½″
4″
½″
STRIPS 1″ WIDE
17⅝″
⁵⁄₈″
17¾″
17⅝″

4

B   A
1″
7″   13½″   9″

5

1″ C
9″
7⅞″

6

1½″
9″
17¾″
1″   1″
FIXED SCREEN

7

8¾″
1″
16½″
1″
DOOR

8

SLIDE
FIXED SCREEN

9

RIDGE
2¼″   2⅛″
1½″   2″
1⅝″
POST
1⁹⁄₁₀″
RIDGE
18¾″
18½″
3″
1″
38¼″
38¼″

- 126 -

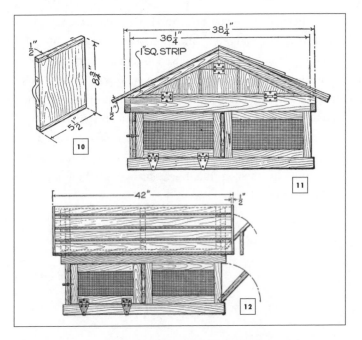

FIGURE 1: FLOOR AND CEILING; FIGURE 3: ARRANGEMENT OF COMPARTMENTS; FIGURE 8: LOWER STORY ASSEMBLED READY FOR ROOF STORY; FIGURE 9: FRAMING OF THE ROOF; FIGURE 11: SIDE VIEW, SHOWING SPACING OF ROOF BOARDS; FIGURE 12: END VIEW, SHOWING TRIM AND DOOR ON GABLE END.

The house is constructed on general building principles. The process outline also follows, in general, the typical methods used in building construction. While the construction is simple, it must be carried out systematically. The house has a framed gable roof, which is rough-boarded and shingled. The interior arrangement is original.

The post should be sunk into the ground about $2\frac{1}{2}$ ft. and set into a concrete foundation, if convenient. This will ensure a more long-term, as well as a more rigid, support. Care should be taken that the post is set plumb; this can be accomplished with the use of a plumb bob. The post should be braced to keep it vertical, particularly if a concrete foundation is poured and tamped around it.

The construction should be painted two coats, inside and out, in a color that harmonizes with buildings or other surroundings.

CHAPTER 5

BATHING BEAUTIES

Just because an animal has feathers doesn't mean it doesn't get dirty. Wild birds have to contend with the dust and dirt from their travels, sticky resins and residues from the plants they frequent and even leftover gunk from feeding on insects. That's why almost all birds enjoy a good bath—and providing a place for bathing is crucial to inviting birds into your yard.

The presence of water—especially clean water with a place nearby to dry off—is a tempting garden feature for just about any type of bird. And a birdbath need not be a formal stone sculpture or something elegant and spectacular to behold. Birds aren't that

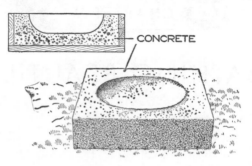

An ordinary washbasin was used to shape the depression in the concrete. As this example shows, concrete makes terrific birdbath material, as does plaster. Both materials are easy to work with, are durable under the assault of the elements all year long, and can be made attractive to suit the style of your garden.

fussy (remember, in the wild, a puddle often serves as a bathtub). The basics of choosing or making a birdbath are simple. It should have enough water for the birds to splash around in but not enough for them to have a swim, and it should be easily accessible, with a place to perch and dry off so that they won't get caught in the water, tire and drown.

The actual container for the water can be incredibly simple. For instance, a concrete worker decided to build a basic, low-lying concrete water basin for the larger birds in his yard. Having no forms at hand, the worker used an ordinary washbasin and a wood box, as shown in the illustration opposite. The basin was greased before being placed in the concrete. The completed concrete basin was buried, its upper surface level with the ground.

A birdbath can also be a wonderful complement to your yard or garden design. No garden can be considered quite complete without a birdbath of some sort, and it need not be an elaborate or expensive affair of concrete or stone to attract the birds. (They are generally more appreciative of the water than of the container.)

This drawing shows a simple design for a birdbath that can be executed quickly and inexpensively. A suitable length of 2 x 2-in. stock is used for the upright support, which is driven into the ground. An earthenware dish such as a

ADVICE FROM A BIRDER If you want to make your birdbath even more attractive to feathered travelers, add a mister or dripping system (available at most large home centers). Birds find moving water much more inviting than still bodies of water. As a bonus, such systems can help keep the water clean.

SEVERAL CONCRETE BIRDBATHS

A concrete birdbath with an attractive pedestal and molded base can be constructed for your backyard if you have some experience creating plaster molds. The pedestal, base and

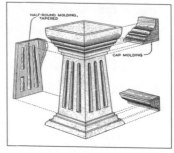

vase are preferably reinforced with wire mesh, and the pedestal may, by using a tapered wooden core, be cast hollow, thus saving material. The whole piece may be cast as a unit, if desired.

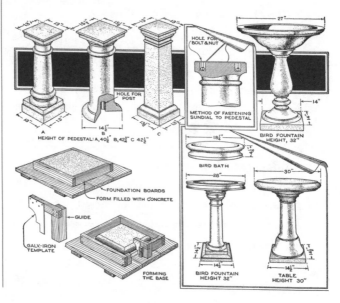

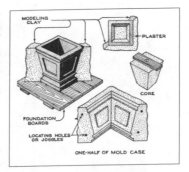

A square bottom-less box of the desired size is placed upon the foundation board; a template is cut from galvanized sheet iron, to the proper shape, and fastened to a wooden board. After the cement has been placed in the box, the template is moved along each side in turn, the material scraped off being carefully removed.

flowerpot, is set in, preferably one about 16 in. in diameter and about 2 in. deep, and used as a container for the water. Four horizontal arms, each 1 ft. long and 1½ in. square, are fastened to the sides of the support to bear the dish. These arms are mortised to make an opening into which the dish is inserted and that prevents it from being pushed off accidentally. Simple brackets underneath the projecting supports can be used to add to the appearance and solidity of the completed bath.

You should let your imagination be your guide in making unusual birdbaths that will function both decoratively and as relief for dirty birds. Any of a number of novel, decorative birdbaths can easily made from ordinary materials and will add charm to any garden or lawn. For the best results, choose a spot away from the

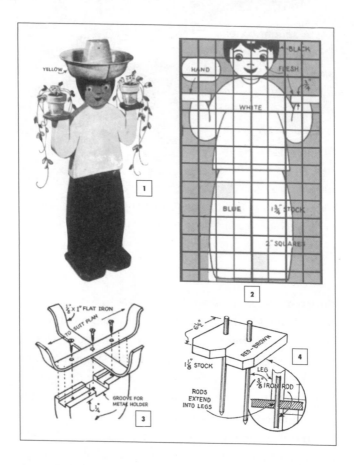

house, against a background of shrubs; a birdbath not only looks best in such a setting, but will also be more attractive to birds. The location should be shaded at least part of the day. The water in small pans will evaporate quickly if left in the sun continually, and the paint will not stand up through a season of blistering sun.

The sombrero shown opposite is really a washbasin with an inverted flowerpot set in it to simulate the tall crown. *Figures 1* to *4* give all the details. A potted plant is held in each hand. The basin is held by two crossed pieces of flat iron. Bend these to the shape of the pan and set them into grooves cut in the head so that the top one rests flush with the top of the head. Fasten with three screws. This arrangement allows the pan to be

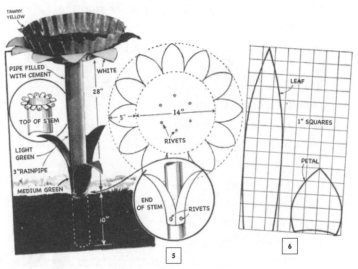

removed for cleaning and filling. Screw the hands and feet in place and drill a hole through each foot and up into each leg for a distance of several inches. Then insert metal rods extending about 10 in. below the base. When these are pushed into the ground, the figure will be held securely.

The huge flower resembling a giant daffodil (*Figures 5* and *6*) from which birds can drink is made entirely of sheet metal. The crinkle-edged water pan is nothing more than a hog-feeding pan. The petals are cut from galvanized sheet iron, and the stem is a length of rain pipe filled with cement. The disk holding the pan is scalloped to form petals. Set the pan inside and bend up three of the petals to hold the pan securely, turning over the tips. Then remove the pan and bend the other petals uniformly, as shown. The top of the rain-pipe stem is serrated and bent so that it can be riveted or soldered to the bottom of the petal piece. Cut three sheet-metal

ADVICE FROM A BIRDER The features of the birdbath you select for your garden will determine, to a degree, what types of birds can and will use the birdbath. If you opt for a large birdbath, make sure it is no deeper than 4 inches or smaller birds will not be able to use it. The ideal model becomes very shallow at the lip and has a rough surface that makes it easy for birds to gain a purchase on the edges without the risk of falling in.

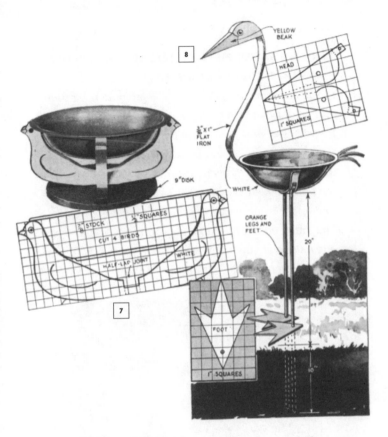

leaves and bend the lower ends to fit around the pipe. Rivet them in position and then bend the tips over. Paint each part before assembling.

Birds may bathe safely in the bath held by four doves, *Figure 7*, if your neighborhood is free from prowling felines. It is especially suitable for a small, informal garden or a secluded corner of a large one. Although the pan used originally was 11 in. in diameter and 2³/4 in.

RUNNING WATER PIPED UP TREE TRUNK SUPPLIES
HANGING BIRDBATH AND FEEDER

Attractive in its simplicity, this combination birdbath and feeder will be a great favorite with your feathered friends. The unit is suspended from a tree limb with wire or chain, and the bath features running water that drips from an overhead outlet. Water is piped to the bath by means of a length of copper tubing stapled to the tree trunk and along the underside of the limb. The lower end of the tubing is connected to the water line as shown; the valve is adjusted for a steady drip. A metal pan for the bath and two cups, one for feed

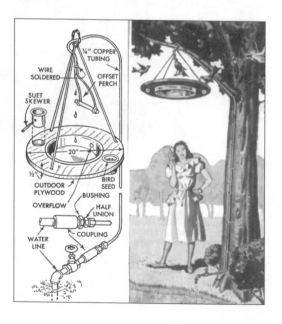

and the other for suet, are set in a circular plywood platform. A hole for an overflow is drilled through the side of the pan just under the platform, and the suet cup is fitted with a skewer to hold the suet cake in place. Another novel feature of this unit is an offset perch made from two pieces of stiff wire and a length of dowel. This is soldered to the end of the copper tubing to permit the birds to catch the water as it drips from the outlet. The copper tubing is painted to match the bark of the tree, and the undersides of the platform, pan and cups are painted the same shade in a mottled effect that blends in with the foliage.

deep, the design may be altered for pans of other sizes. The two pieces are half-lapped at the center, glued and nailed, then attached to a round base about 9 in. in diameter. If desired, however, the base may be mounted on a suitable pedestal. The doves are white; the feet, bills and outline of the wings purple; and the base is a deep green or reddish brown. The pan is light green, and the eyes are a couple of black or red thumbtacks.

The long neck and legs of the crane, *Figure 8*, are formed from flat iron. The feet and head are made from sheet metal. The body is a water basin. Point the end of the neck piece to make the top of the bill, and bend the main part of the piece to the contour of the basin. Then split the other end to make a tail. Shape another piece of iron to extend just to the rim of the pan, place it across

BIRDBATH FITTED WITH TRAPEZE
PLEASES FEATHERED BATHERS

If you have a birdbath in your garden, rig up a trapeze above it. The enjoyment that the birds will get from this will more than repay you for your time. Just bend a length of small brass rod into a U-shape and invert it above the water. From this, suspend a miniature swing made from fine brass wire.

and under the first piece and rivet them together. Use iron rods for legs, flattening and bending them to join the crosspiece, to which they are riveted. Cut the head from galvanized sheet metal, bend it to fit over the beak and rivet the tabs at each side to the back of the neck. To hold it even more securely, a stove bolt may be run through the eyes. The legs are pushed through holes in the sheet-metal feet and extend into the ground.

Because painted objects—especially those done in bright, gay colors—have a tendency to fade quickly, it is best to use outdoor paints recommended as having fast, durable colors. Also, outside pieces such as these should be given two or three coats of paint and a finishing coat of spar varnish so that they withstand the weather. Of course, garden ornaments should always be stored inside during the winter months.

Regardless of the birdbath design you choose, you must keep it clean if you are to keep the birds coming back. Just like us, no bird wants to roll around in muck. Change the water in your birdbath every day during the season, and use a scrub brush regularly to remove algae and debris from the basin so that birds always find clean and refreshing facilities whenever they frequent your yard.

KEEPING THE BIRDS AT HOME IN YOUR GARDEN

The chances of attracting birds—and keeping them around—increase if you provide readily accessible water. Where water quickly evaporates from a shallow dish, a constant supply can be maintained by using inverted flasks or jugs held a short distance about the bottom of the pans or dishes. Take the simple type of birdbath shown

here: A large, shallow dish, preferably light green in color, is set on a stump or pedestal, and a gallon jug of

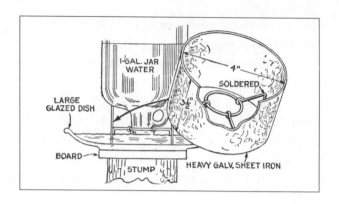

water, fitted with a sheet-metal collar, is inverted in the center of the dish, as shown above. The collar is wide enough to keep the mouth of the jug above the bottom, and a wire frame in the collar holds the jug securely in position. The result is a constant supply of water until the jug is empty. The same principle is used in making the small sugar-water feeder, below. In this case, a flask or bottle is used as the reservoir, while the pan is covered with a perforated cover to minimize evaporation. The cover should be located just above the level of the liquid so that birds will have no difficulty getting at it. A

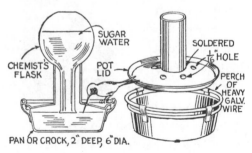

California bird lover succeeded in attracting hundreds of hummingbirds to his grounds by using such feeders. For hummingbirds, the feeder should be arranged so

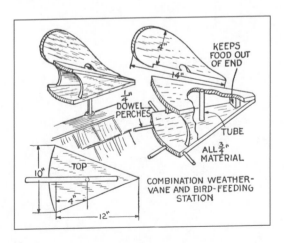

KEEPS FOOD OUT OF END

¼" DOWEL PERCHES

TUBE

ALL ¾" MATERIAL

TOP

COMBINATION WEATHER-VANE AND BIRD-FEEDING STATION

that the birds have access to the liquid while on the wing, as they seldom alight. The detail at the bottom of page 143 shows a protected feeding shelter in which crumbs can be placed. The shelter is pivoted to rotate, and the vane on top keeps it pointed into the wind. Keeping the feeder supplied with crumbs is easy if you use a long stick or pole with a can nailed to the top end.

CHAPTER 6

PROTECTING FEATHERED FRIENDS

I t's a dangerous world out there when you're a tiny little feathered creature. It seems the smaller and more fragile a bird is, the more potential enemies it has. It's a simple fact of nature: Birds don't lack for predators that think they make tasty meals or want to make eggs or hatchlings a part of their diet. But the threats don't just come from predatory animals. Just as in other groups that make up the animal kingdom, there is hard-fought competition among birds (and the favorites of backyard bird-watching are inevitably on the short end of that battle). And as if all that weren't enough, the man-made structures that form our neighborhoods can create surprising dangers for birds on the wing. So making a welcoming, bird-friendly environment in the yard or garden means offering protection from the various threats small birds face.

CATS

Cats are one of the chief dangers to backyard birds. Cats love to stalk and attack small birds and will not hesitate to strike birds in their nests, in birdhouses, on the ground or even at a feeder. Even well-fed cats will hunt birds—it's simply what they are wired to do. The first and most simple line of defense is to keep your cat indoors. Of course, this doesn't protect birds from other neighborhood cats. If yours is an outdoor cat, use a bell attached to the cat's collar to alert birds to its presence. But you should never underestimate the stealth and cunning of a house cat (keep in mind that they are, however distantly, related to the lions that quietly prowl the savannah). Some experts recommend positioning a birdhouse or feeder right in front of a window so that the cat

ADVICE FROM A BIRDER Cats hate water. This makes a surprising spray one of the best ways to deter cats in the yard from stalking birds. If you have the time and vigilance, you can wait for the cat to show up near a birdhouse or feeder and spray the cat with a hose. If that becomes impractical, you can set up a motion-activated sprinkler near where birds congregate to surprise the cat when it goes hunting. Usually, one or two shocking showers will teach a cat to avoid the area around a feeder, bath or birdhouse.

A CAT-PROOF BIRD TABLE

This bird table is a source of great enjoyment for its owners, particularly since this garden ornament's constructions makes birds feel secure from cats and other enemies. The sketch shows the arrangement of the table braced at the top of a 6-ft. post. Shrubbery surrounds the table, and a light evergreen climber clings to the post yet does not give the cats a good foothold.

Experience has taught these homeowners that area birds prefer bread crumbs and cracked wheat to other varieties of food. The linnets are especially fond of oranges. The owners cut an orange in two and place the halves on the table; they are rewarded—and amused— by the birds that arrive to balance on one side of the orange while pecking at the fruit. Soon the orange peel is almost entirely emptied. After you provide the table with a small basin of fresh water, the birds use it as a drinking cup as well as a bathtub.

MAKE A BIRD FEEDER CAT- AND SQUIRREL-PROOF WITH A CAN LID

Finding that squirrels were robbing a bird feeder set up in his backyard, one home-owner stopped the trouble by mounting a garbage can lid on the standard of the feeder as shown. The lid is also effective in preventing cats from climbing the post to catch birds.

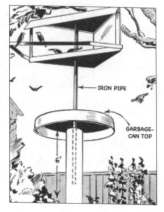

can act on its stalking urges from behind the safety of a pane of glass. Don't invite stray cats into your yard by leaving any kind of food source outdoors. If they become a serious problem anyway, you can use a live trap to catch stray or feral cats. Contact your local ASPCA or similar organization for trap information.

SQUIRRELS

Squirrels are more likely to raid birds' nests or birdhouses to eat the eggs (full-grown adult birds can put up too much of a fight for the average squirrel to contend with). They will also try to break into bird feeders and feast on the seeds inside. Squirrels tend to weigh less and be more acrobatic than house cats, so they are usually more of a problem for nests or birdhouses in trees or on weak supports, such as a hanging wire between a house and a tree. The best way to deter squirrels is to block their access to the birdhouse or feeder.

For instance, to prevent squirrels from scrambling up a birdhouse standard or tree to get at a birdhouse, take a length of stovepipe and slip it over the standard or tree trunk as indicated. Because the surface of the pipe is hard and slick, the squirrel will not be able to grip it well enough to climb it. If the standard or tree trunk is too large or too small for the pipe, substitute a piece of sheet metal.

Squirrels like to steal from exposed nests or nesting areas that are within easy striking distance. This means that any birdhouse in a tree is a potential target for squirrels. And even if they don't succeed in snatching eggs, their efforts can dislodge a hanging birdhouse, sending it crashing to the ground. That's why mounting a birdhouse or feeder on the side of a house or garage—or another flat, inaccessible surface—is often the best solution to foiling predatory squirrels. Of course, certain species of birds won't nest in a structure that can be attached to a wall.

As an alternative, you can mount just about any type of birdhouse on a wooden or metal pole. A smooth metal pole offers the best resistance to climbing predators, but homeowners may find the solution a bit ugly. However, even if you choose a wood post or rustic-looking wood log, you can take steps to stop any threats from climbing hunters. The trick is to either block a climber's progress up the pole or create a surface that won't allow climbers to gain a purchase.

One such effective guard can be created by cutting the bottom out of a large plastic bottle, then tying the bottle to a feeder pole. Simple as it is, it's sure to work against

---

DISHPAN CAT AND SQUIRREL GUARD FOR BIRDHOUSE

An effective guard that protects birdhouses and feeding tables from cat or squirrel raids can be made from an old dishpan. Turn the pan upside down and cut three slits in the center. Turn the metal between the cuts back to form ears from which the device can be nailed to the pole. When the birdhouse is protected in this manner, a cat or other villain cannot reach the top of the pole and disturb the residents or visitors.

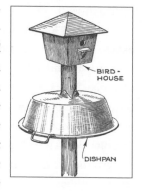

squirrel thieves. Another simple guard can be constructed by building a band of tin a foot wide around a solitary tree trunk.

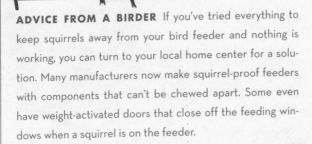

BAND OF TIN AROUND TREE PREVENTS CATS AND, SQUIRRELS CLIMBING UP TO BIRD HOUSE

12"

48"

Similar and somewhat more aesthetically pleasing solutions can be found in home centers and stores that carry birdhouses. These include functional and decorative shields that are easy to install and available in many different materials.

You can also make any pole inaccessible to four-legged bird hunters by smearing it with oil or petroleum jelly liberally mixed with red pepper or chili sauce. After one encounter with the substance, the predators will find someplace else to look for food. Lastly, if the problem persists, you can use a chemical squirrel repellant that emits a smell that will repulse squirrels without affecting the birds.

SQUIRREL-PROOF A BIRD FEEDER

Suspend a coffee can from three wires attached to the bird feeder bottom and you can keep unwanted poachers from eating birdseed. It swings if touched, thus causing squirrels to lose their grip, protecting your feathered friends' seeds.

Screw eyes

2-lb. coffee can, both ends removed

DOGS

Cats aren't the only house pets that can do damage to birds and bird-attracting yard features. The family dog can create fear and havoc for nesting birds (especially ground-nesting species). Although not a natural bird hunter (except for actual "bird dogs"—and they tend to look for dead game and something heartier than the backyard bluebird), a rambunctious dog can chase and scare off birds in the yard and make a deadly game of rag doll toss out of any chick that has fallen out of a nest. Dogs are also likely to consider a birdbath their own private water dish and may knock over lighter or unsecured baths. Whenever birds are nesting in the backyard, keep dogs inside, or at least chained or otherwise restricted so that they can't disturb the birds, feeders or baths.

SLITHERING EGG STEALERS

In addition to the four-legged predators, other hunters are looking to make a snack out of your backyard bird population. In many parts of the country, snakes are always ready to munch on birds' eggs and can quietly empty a nest. The solution is the same as for cats and squirrels—stop the predator from reaching the birdhouse or nest. If you have snakes about, keep nesting boxes and birdhouses out of trees. Anything that blocks a pole or positions the birdhouse on a surface that snakes can't reach will do the trick. But stop short of poisoning, trapping or otherwise hurting the slithering creatures—they're an important part of the natural ecosystem, so deterrence is the preferred method of control.

RACCOONS AND OPOSSUMS

Raccoons and opossums also have a taste for birds' eggs and hatchlings and will raid birdhouses and nests wherever they can reach them (which, particularly for raccoons, is just about anywhere). Fortunately, you can protect eggs and hatchlings from the pillaging claws of these raiders by using any number of predator guards currently on the market. These devices are attached over the hole of a birdhouse and make it more difficult for predators to reach in and raid the nest—a purchase to consider if you live near woods or in an area where wildlife proliferates.

If the birds in your yard have made their own nests in your trees, you'll have to be a little more stringent in your efforts to persuade the local wildlife to stay away

TIPPING BIRDBATH ATTRACTS SONGBIRDS AND KEEPS CATS AWAY

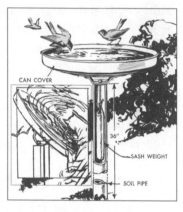

Do you want a bird-bath to attract song-birds and at the same time save the birds from prowling cats? This tipping birdbath will serve both pur-poses. A 5-ft. length of soil pipe is set in the ground so that 3 ft. of it projects above the surface. The bowl of the bath, which is a garbage can lid, is held on the base by a sash weight tied to the han-dle and suspended inside the soil pipe. When a cat attempts to get at birds in the bath, the cover tips and spills water on it. The sudden loss of support, plus the unexpected bath, will discourage even the most persis-tent cat. The sash weight will right the cover as soon as the cat runs away. To decorate, the soil pipe and gar-bage can cover may be painted a bright color, and stones and colored bits of pottery may be cemented around the soil pipe.

PIPING RACCOONS OUT OF THE NEST

The pilfering claws of raccoons can spell disaster for the eggs and the young birds in a birdhouse sanctuary, but it's a simple matter to deter these deadly bandits from ruining  *your backyard aviary. Attach a plumbing pipe flange and short length of pipe—2 in. will suffice—over the hole in your birdhouse. The diameter of the flange and pipe should be as close to the diameter of the hole as possible, and slightly larger if a perfect match cannot be made. You can use metal or PVC pipe, but the plastic variety will weather better. Once in place, the pipe creates a tunnel through which birds can easily enter and leave, but which will frustrate the greedy grasp of a hungry raccoon.*

from the eggs. A highly effective—if slightly pricey—solution is an ultrasound predator device. Motion activated, it puts out a high-frequency sound that birds and humans can't hear, but that will drive raccoons and opossums (and dogs, cats and squirrels) crazy. Although ultrasound units are very effective, you can get almost the same amount of protection by using a raccoon repellant such as coyote urine (available through some home centers and mail-order retailers) or other natural or synthetic chemical repellant. The downside to these is that they need to be regularly reapplied or they won't remain effective.

BIRD BULLIES

Unfortunately, birds don't need to look beyond their own corner of the animal kingdom to find enemies. Smaller birds such as bluebirds are subject to attack from certain types of sparrows and starlings, which will attempt to drive out or even kill other, more timid birds. Aggressive species such as crows, blue jays and grackles will attempt to overpower other species, especially during the nesting season, when they are known to destroy nests and eggs and fight for territory. But the same love of nature that drives you to create a welcoming backyard environment for birds prevents you from doing much about bird-on-bird attacks. Laws are strict about killing birds (outside of those such as duck and pheasants that are seasonally hunted). Only the rock pigeon, the house sparrow and the European starling are allowed to be killed by a homeowner in most states.

Ethically—and usually legally as well—you simply have to let nature take its course, even if that course means losing the presence of some favorite songbirds.

An ironic downside to creating a welcoming haven for birds in your yard is that the more successful you are—the more birds visit your yard—the more your yard can become a target hunting ground for the bigger birds of prey. Although it may be disturbing to see a kite or hawk swoop down and snatch a smaller songbird, you should consider this part of your bird-watching experience. It is, after all, a integral part of a healthy ecosystem, and there is virtually no means of preventing predation from larger birds.

PIRACY BELLS FOR BIRD FEEDER

You can prevent piracy around your bird-feeding station by hanging bells over the tray, as shown in the illustration. Small birds will slip between the bells and feed undisturbed, but squirrels or large birds will hit the bells and be frightened off by the noise.

THE MAN-MADE WORLD

Predators aren't the only things feathered visitors have to worry about in your yard. Birds are also at risk from man-made obstacles—most often windows. Each year, an amazing numbers of birds fall victim to a reflection in window glass. Birds get fooled into thinking their own reflections are enemies encroaching on their territory, or even potential mates, and will fly full speed into the image, risking injury and even death. The easiest way to prevent this is to block the windows with bird netting; you can also use decals or other surface decorations to break up the surface of the glass and prevent reflections.

ADVICE FROM THE BIRDER Sadly, many of the solutions to prevent birds from hitting windows are simply not very attractive. But you're not forced to choose between songbird safety and spoiling the view from your picture window. One good solution are stained-glass suncatchers. Hung inside the window, they sparkle and display different colors, warning birds away from the windows while creating an effect quite pleasing to the human eye.

CHAPTER 7

SPOTTING
BIRDS

The whole idea behind tempting birds into your yard and garden is that it allows you to enjoy their beauty. And although songbirds bring with them the beauty of song, the heart and soul of birding is observing and noting the interesting behavior and varied markings that distinguish different species of avian life. Although not all birds sing—and a few even make rather unpleasant sounds—all birds are worth watching for what they do and how they are dressed. The natural complement to close observation is, of course, recording what you see. That's why journaling about your observations is a natural and extremely enjoyable extension of the pastime of bird-watching.

Bird-watching begins with spotting the species that are visiting your surroundings. If you've properly prepared your own little bird environment with water (for both bathing and drinking), food and housing, you'll likely attract a range of birds. It is very difficult to get close enough to see interesting details and not disrupt their activities without using a pair of good quality binoculars. You don't necessarily have to recognize or identify different birds to enjoy bird-watching; beautiful plumage will be beautiful even if you don't know the name of the bird, and the fascination often lies in the surprising habits of any given individual. So while one of the excellent bird

guides available on bookstore shelves is a good (but not essential) purchase, you will definitely enjoy bird-watching more if you have a decent pair of binoculars.

CHOOSING A NEW PAIR OF EYES

The first thing you'll discover when shopping for binoculars is the amazing range of choices available. Of course, your selection will most likely be limited by expense: Binoculars range widely in price, and the models at the very high end can fetch a month's salary or more. Beginners, however, need only a sturdy pair to cover all their viewing needs. With the right handling, even a modestly priced pair will last for decades.

When selecting binoculars, you'll first consider the three primary factors that affect what you see: magnification, lighting and visual field. These three are interrelated. For instance, great magnification often means a smaller visual field, so choosing wisely among these is a matter of balancing the factors.

Magnification, or the binoculars' "power," is simply a measure of how many times the view is magnified. The number is usually placed on the shell of the binoculars— for example, "7x" designates 7 times magnification over normal sight. If you are planning to watch birds at a great remove, a higher magnification will be a boon to making out the details of plumage and markings. Depending on the model and how much you're willing to spend,

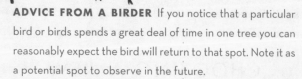

you can buy a pair of binoculars of 10x or even 15x magnification and well beyond. The higher the magnification, the more expensive the binoculars will be, because maintaining quality across the surface of the lens is a greater challenge as magnification increases. However, the higher the magnification, the more "hand shake" becomes a factor. That's why, for most beginners and backyard enthusiasts, 7x or 8x magnification is plenty.

Lighting or illumination describes how much light the binoculars take in, which in turn determines how much detail you can see—especially in low-light areas such as a shady grove of trees. The number that describes the light-grabbing abilities of any

given model is simply the binoculars' front lens size. For instance, just as on a camera, a 35-mm. lens is going to capture less light than a 50-mm. lens. The lens size is usually tagged on as a suffix to the magnification marked on the binoculars, so "7x35" represents a pair of binoculars with 7 times magnification and a 35-mm lens. For beginners, a 35- or 50-mm. lens should accommodate most viewing conditions. If your yard is in deep shade or you regularly watch night birds, go with a bigger lens size.

When viewing birds, you need enough area in the visual field to locate the subject and follow its movement. This visual field, or as binoculars makers call it, field of view, is generally measured as the number of feet you can see side to

ADVICE FROM A BIRDER Binoculars have several different lenses and mirrors between the outer lens and eyepiece. The configuration and type of lenses used determine magnification and other qualities. To prevent glare and minimize the loss of light coming into the binoculars, choose a model with coated lenses. The lens coating will prevent glare and reduce the amount of light reflected back out of the binoculars. Be sure that the lens coating has been applied to the interior lenses as well as the front lens and eyepiece.

side at 1,000 yards. The greater the visual field, the easier it will be to locate a bird in the surroundings. The field of view measurement is usually included with the binoculars' specs. Although it's tempting for the first timer to choose wide-angle binoculars, well-constructed wide-angle lenses are expensive, and inexpensive wide-angle binoculars can be very frustrating because their focus will vary across the space of the lens. For backyard viewing, you should be fine with a pair of binoculars with a normal, rather than a wide-angle, field of view.

In your search for the right pair of binoculars, you'll encounter different functional designs. There are two basic types: roof prism and Porro prism; there is also a style known as reverse Porro prism. Porro prism is the more traditional design; such binoculars are usually bulkier and heavier, with refined light characteristics and superior depth of field. Roof-prism binoculars are often more streamlined (the barrels are actually straight

ADVICE FROM A BIRDER If you're planning to wear your eyeglasses while bird watching, be sure try out binoculars with your glasses on. Look for binoculars with "long eye relief"—a design that provides a space for eyeglasses between where the eye focuses behind the eyepiece and the first set of internal lenses.

instead of tapered) and are generally more weatherproof than other types, which makes them pricier (but essential if you do a lot of bird-watching in inclement weather). Reverse-Porro models are usually more compact than the other types, making them easy to use and carry. They tend toward the less expensive end of the price scale.

Regardless of the type of binoculars you're considering, you can test them before you buy them by aiming them at a piece of paper on a pole, tree or the side of a building. As you focus in on the paper, any lettering should be as crisp at the edges of the lens as it is in the middle. If you look at a light source, the lens should be as bright at the edges as it is in the middle. If the edge of the lens appears to be a different color, reject the binoculars: That's a sign of inferior lenses.

You should also become familiar with the focusing mechanism of the pair you choose—before you buy them. If you can't figure it out, have a salesperson instruct you in the proper use of the glasses so that you aren't stuck trying to figure out the technology when you desperately want to see a bird in your yard.

Just as important as selecting the right pair of binoculars is taking care of the pair you buy. Handle your binoculars carefully, because one good rap can put the barrels out of alignment, a situation that requires a professional's skill to remedy. Keep the binoculars in their case when not in use, and try to keep them dry at all times—if water gets into the interior of the unit, it can ruin the optics.

You also want to avoid scratching the lenses. Don't stand the binoculars on a surface with the lenses down. Clean the lenses with a soft lens brush (available at camera stores), or use lens paper to carefully remove obvious dirt. If the lenses are smudged, use a lens-cleaning solution with camera lens paper.

A good pair of binoculars will aid you in identifying birds that visit your yard and will help you discover the fascinating habits and behaviors of those birds.

KEEPING A JOURNAL

Whether you use binoculars, a spotting scope or just your eyes, you can increase your bird-watching enjoyment by logging your finds in a journal. A bird-watching journal can be as simple as a notebook with descriptions of the birds you've seen or as complex as a large sketchbook with detailed listings about the time, date and location you saw the bird, the type of bird you saw, what you saw it doing and even sketches of the bird.

ADVICE FROM A BIRDER Don't just look for birds; look for predators as well. Although many predators will cause birds to flee, some will inspire amazing behavior on the birds' part. For instance, a red-breasted nuthatch will often defend its nest against a squirrel's encroachment by positioning itself on the tree trunk—facing downward—and doing a slow, rhythmic dance that stops the squirrel in its tracks. Antipredator tactics can be some of the most intriguing bird-watching around.

Start out slowly and use the journal to capture basic descriptions that will help you identify the bird in a guidebook later. You can build up to the kind of detailed list that more experienced birders compile to keep track of the species they have witnessed over time.

Journaling allows you to go back and remember your big discoveries (like the time you finally saw a yellow-bellied sapsucker), builds a sense of anticipation about what you might find and gives you a way to interact with other birders through comparing notes about what birds you've seen where. The exercise of filling out a journal will also help you to become precise in your observations, ultimately helping you get more out of the time you spend watching birds.

INDEX

Acorn wren house, 102–103

Aerial displays
    as courtship rituals, 25–26
    by raptors, 15

American dippers, 69

Autumn
    birds of Halloween, 48
    birds on ground, 29
    feed for, 42–43
    physiological adaptations for
        cold weather and, 51
    preparing for migration,
        42–49. See also Migration
    removing nests or not, 43
    subtle changes in birds, 43–49

Bark and bark-covered bird
    houses, 111–112, 113–114

Berries, 17, 19, 93–95, 114

Binoculars, 161–166

Birdbaths, 129–144
    attracting birds to, 131
    cleaning, 20
    complementing landscaping,
        131
    depth of, 136
    design impacting species
        attracted, 136
    designing, 133–134
    finishes for, 140–141
    general guidelines for, 129–130
    misters/drip systems in, 131
    models of. See Birdbaths
        (models)
    for smaller birds, 143
    territorial nature of birds
        and, 99

Birdbaths (models)
    brick/cement wheel, 20–21
    concrete models, 132–133
    with constant water supply,
        138, 141–142
    crane bath, 137, 139–141

daffodil bath, 135, 136–137
dove-held bath, 137–139
quick, inexpensive earthen-
    ware model, 131–133
sombrero bath, 134, 135
tipping birdbath, 154
trapeze in, 140
tree-hanging water-fed bath,
    138
washbasin-formed concrete,
    130–131

Bird feeders. See also Birdhouses;
    Feeding and food; Wren
    houses
    attracting birds to, 86–87,
        89–94
    attracting birds with, 72–73,
        74, 76
    cat-proof bird table, 147
    cleaning, 19–20, 87–89
    decorative value of, 78–79
    eggshells in, 16
    fruit feeders, 92–93
    irruption and, 76
    keeping full through winter,
        49–50
    keeping predators from.
        See Protecting birds
    ladder hoist for heavy pole
        feeders, 88–89
    location of, 84–85
    materials for, 79
    models of. See Bird feeders
        (models)
    piracy bells for, 157
    platform feeders, 74
    safety of, 84–85
    tending, 86–89
    territorial nature of birds
        and, 99
    tubular feeders, 75–76
    types of, 73–79

winter feeders, 44–47
for winter snacks, 60–61
Bird feeders (models)
cafeteria feeder, 52–53
coat-hanger feeder, 75
feeding tray, 81
gourd feeders, 87
hopper-type feeders, 44, 77
hummingbird feeders,
76–78, 82, 142–144
mixing-bowls feeder, 85
pan nailed to tree, 80
pheasant feeders from milk
cans, 73
pivoting post winter feeder, 60
quickie clothesline feeder, 86
sill-type feeder, 56
sliding feeder, 61
split-keg feeder, 78
tin-can feeder, 75
vane-type feeders, 44–45,
56–57
Birdhouses
attracting birds to, 97, 114
bird species and, 98–100
cement, 116–120
custom designs, 121–124
detachable, 120
deterring squirrels from
raiding, 148–151
finishes for, 121
getting birds to use, 109
inaugurating, 97
not getting used, 109
predator guards for, 99
rough, rugged, rustic,
110–115
territorial nature of birds
and, 99
Birdhouses (models). See also
Wren houses
bark and bark-covered
houses, 111–112, 113–114
cement models, 116–120

clay-flowerpot houses, 33
firewood-slab house, 111
hanging log house, 110–111
helmet-houses, 115
hollow-log, 26–27, 110–111,
112, 114
martin birdhouse, 124. See
also Purple martin houses
miniature summer house,
113
modeling your home, 121–124
nesting shelf, 46
octagonal four-compartment,
46–47
pigeon house, 125–128
spanning garden high post
gate, 18
sparrow-proof martin house, 116
straw-hat house, 110
thatched-roof cabin, 112
Birding. See also Identifying birds
about: overview of, 159–161
attracting birds and, 160. See
also Bird feeders; Birdbaths;
Birdhouses; Garden
attraction of, 9–10
in autumn. See Autumn;
Migration
binoculars for, 161–166
creating welcoming environment
for, 10–12
discretion for, 160
field guides, 17, 59
gardening and. See Garden
getting started, 17
growth of juveniles and, 35–39
"Hands off!" advice for, 30
late in year, 41
observing predators while, 167
spring migration and, 13–15.
See also Mating; Spring
routine
in summer, 35–40
in winter. See Winter

Birds of prey. *See* Raptors (birds of prey)
Bluebirds, 30, 46–47, 83, 112, 118, 156
Blue jays. *See* Jays
Caches of food, 58–59, 71
Cafeteria feeder, 52–53
Calcium, 16, 79
Cardinals, 42, 56, 81, 92–93
Carrion eaters, 66
Castle wren house, 102
Cat-proof bird table, 147
Cats, protecting birds from, 146–148, 154
Cement (concrete)
    birdbaths, 132–133
    birdhouses, 116–120
Clay flowerpots
    as birdbaths, 131–133
    as birdhouses, 33
Cleaning feeders, boxes, birdbaths, 19–20, 87–89
Clothesline feeder, 86. *See also* Sliding feeder
Coat-hanger feeder, 75
Coconut-shell wren house, 100
Cold weather. *See* Autumn; Winter
Concrete. *See* Cement (concrete)
Condors, 65, 66
Corn, protecting, 93
Courtship rituals, 25–26. *See also* Mating
Crane birdbath, 137, 139–141
Crows, 25, 32, 48, 50, 55, 71, 156
Cuckoos, 31, 50
Daffodil birdbath, 136–137
Dances. *See* Aerial displays
Dogs, protecting birds from, 152
Dove-held birdbath, 137–139
Doves, 47, 83, 91. *See also* Pigeon house
Ducks, 25, 50, 156
Eagles, 9, 34, 66, 68

Eggs. *See also* Mating
    fertilizing and laying, 34–35
    hatching, 34, 35
    keeping hands off, 30
    keeping predators from. *See* Protecting birds
    mimicking host's eggs, 31
Falcons, 66
Feeding and food. *See also* Bird feeders
    bulk-up diet, 42
    caches of food, 58–59, 71
    calcium and, 16, 79
    in cold months, 42–43, 59, 62
    diet types and, 63–64
    eggshells (calcium) in feeders, 16, 79
    food for feeders, 80–84
    free lunches, 56
    insect eaters, 70–72
    irruption and, 76
    organic solutions, 91
    preparing for migration and, 48
    raptors and, 64–69
    seed mixes, 80–84, 91
    suet, 11, 42, 45, 75, 83–84, 114, 139
Field guides, 17, 59
Firewood-slab birdhouse, 111
Fledglings, 30, 39
Flycatchers, 15, 50
Flying
    height of, during migration, 51
    process of learning, 30, 37–39
Fruit, birds and, 92–95
Garden, 16–22
    birdbaths complementing, 131
    birdhouse spanning high post gate, 18
    optimizing bird-watching in, 22
    organic, safety and, 91
    planting to attract birds, 16–19, 89–92, 93–94

protecting corn from birds, 93

protecting plants from birds, 94–96

servicing bird feeders, nesting boxes, birdbaths, 19–20

Goldfinches, 16, 42, 76, 83, 98

Gourd feeders, 87

Halloween, birds of, 48

"Hands off!" advice, 30

Hatchlings
getting out of eggs, 34, 35
growth of, 35–37
protection for, 31, 153

Hawks, 15, 32, 50, 53, 66, 67, 157

Helmets, birdhouses from, 115

Hollow-log birdhouses, 26–27, 110–111, 112, 114

Hopper-type feeders, 44, 77

Hummingbird feeders, 76–78, 82, 142–144

Hummingbirds, 17–19, 51, 61, 83, 91

Identifying birds
birds of prey. See Raptors (birds of prey)
comparing and contrasting birds, 38
distinctive behaviors and, 25
field guides and, 17, 59
noting markings and, 38
by sight, 17, 25, 38
by sound, 23

Injured birds, treating, 14, 50

Insect eaters, 70–72

Irruption, 76

Jays, 32, 39, 42, 55, 58, 71, 79, 81, 83, 93, 156

Journal, 166–167
benefits of, 167
complementing close observation, 159

noting birds, then identifying, 17, 23, 38
range of options for, 166
starting out slowly, 167
tracking time/date of sightings, 53

Juvenile birds, growth of, 35–39

Kites, 66, 157

Ladder hoist for heavy pole feeders, 88–89

Lighthouse, 104–105

Log (hollow) birdhouses, 26–27, 110–111

Log (hollow) cement birdhouse, 118–119

Mating. See also Nest(s)
birds flying into windows and, 24
courtship rituals, 25–26
fertilizing, laying eggs, 34–35. See also Eggs
food gathering after, 35
growth of juveniles after, 35–39
marking territory and, 22–25
parental roles, 34–35
process of, 26–35
songs, sounds and, 22–25

Migration
aerial displays during, 15
bird-watching during, 49–53
flight patterns, 50–53
height of flight patterns, 51
irruption and, 76
preparing for, 40, 42–49
return from Central/South America, 14–15
reverse, in spring, 13–15
scope for seeing birds during, 51–52

Milk-can feeders, 73

Miniature summer house, 113

Mixing-bowls feeder, 85

Mockingbirds, 47, 94

Molting, 16, 36, 40, 43
Mud puddles, for nests, 23
Nesting boxes, cleaning, 19–20
Nesting shelf, 46
Nest(s). *See also* Eggs; Mating
  birds returning to, 43
  building, 28–34
  definitions and types of, 30,
    32–34
  fall clean-up and, 43
  finding, 28, 31–32
  ground as, 32
  growth of nestlings and,
    35–37
  "Hands off!" advice for, 30
  juveniles leaving, 37–39
  keeping predators from. *See*
    Protecting birds
  mating process and, 26–35
  providing mud for, 23
  squatters, 30, 31
Noah's ark, 103–104
Nuthatches, 42, 43, 46, 55, 70,
  72, 76, 91, 167
Octagonal four-compartment
  house, 46–47
Opossums and raccoons,
  protecting from, 153–155
Orioles, 50, 92
Owls, 30, 48, 55, 59, 65, 66–67
Pan nailed to tree, 80
Pellets of food, 65
Permanent-resident birds
  reemerging in spring, 15–16
  watching, in winter, 54–59
  winter plumage, 58
Pheasant feeders, 73
Pheasants, 73, 156
Phoebes, 46, 114
Pigeon house, 125–128
Planting to attract birds.
  See Garden
Predators. *See* Protecting birds;
  Raptors (birds of prey)

Protecting birds, 145–158
  about: overview of, 145
  from bully birds, 156–157
  from cats, 146–148, 154
  from dogs, 152
  feeder location and, 84–85
  from flying into windows,
    24, 158
  from man-made objects, 158
  observing predators and, 167
  from raccoons and
    opossums, 153–155
  from snakes, 153
  from squirrels, 148–152
Purple martin houses, 111,
  116, 117–118, 124
Purple martins, 46, 72
Quail, 32, 73, 92
Quickie clothesline feeder, 86
Raccoons and opossums,
  protecting from, 153–155
Raptors (birds of prey), 64–69.
  See also specific raptors
  aerial displays by, 15
  carrion eaters, 66
  characteristics and groups
    of, 65–69
  defined, 65
  food pellets made by, 65
  prey of, 67–69
  talons and fighting ability, 66
  vision of, 66
Ravens, 48. *See also* Crows
Robins, 23, 24, 46, 55, 83, 92–93,
  96, 111
Scarlet tanager, 16
Shivering, 58
Sill-type feeder, 56
Sliding feeder, 61. *See also*
  Clothesline feeder
Snakes, protecting birds from, 153
Sombrero birdbath, 134, 135
Songs and sounds
  changes in patterns, 43–49

marking territory with, 22–25
noting, then identifying
    birds, 23
purposes of, 22
Sparrow-proof martin house, 116
Sparrows, 22, 24, 54, 55, 59,
    91, 113, 156
Split-keg feeder, 78
Spotting scopes, 51. *See also*
    Binoculars
Spring routine, 13–35. *See also*
    Eggs; Mating; Nest(s)
aerial displays by raptors, 15
overwintering resident
    birds emerging, 15–16
reverse migration, 13–15
Squirrels, protecting birds
    from, 148–152
Starlings, 55, 156
Stashes of food, 58–59, 71
Straw-hat birdhouse, 110
Suet, 11, 42, 45, 75, 83–84,
    114, 139
Summer routine, 35–40
Swallows, 22, 23, 25, 30, 40,
    47, 50, 72, 98–99, 111
Tanagers, 16, 91
Territorial actions, 22–25, 99, 156
Thatched-roof cabin birdhouse,
    112
Thrushes, 31, 59, 70
Tin-can feeder, 75
Tipping birdbath, 154
Titmice, 22, 42, 58, 83
Trapeze, in birdbath, 140
Tree-hanging water-fed birdbath,
    138
Vane-type feeders, 44–45, 56–57
Vultures, 48, 66
Warblers, 14–15, 40, 50
Water ouzel, 69
Weather vane feeder.
    See Vane-type feeders
Windmill wren house, 100–101

Windows, birds flying into, 14,
    24, 158
Winter
bird feeders, 60–61. *See also*
    Bird feeders
birds fluffing coat for
    warmth, 55–58
bird-watching, 53, 54–62
cached-food birds and, 58–59
city bird-watching, 55
destination spots, 59–62
dressing warmly in, 54
permanent-resident birds,
    54–59
physiological adaptations for,
    51
shivers in, 58
snow, footprints, and
    birding, 62
Woodpeckers, 25, 42, 46, 71, 81,
    93, 113, 118
Wren houses, 100–109
acorn, 102–103
from auto casing, 32
castle, 102
cement model, 119–120
coconut-shell, 100
entrance hole size, 98
hanging, 103
insulated metal with card-
    board/wood, 105–109
lighthouse, 104–105
Noah's ark, 103–104
octagonal four-compartment,
    46
with pull-out floor, 29
rustic split twig box, 47
springy porch on, 98
windmill, 100–101
Wrens, 28, 30, 71–72

ALSO AVAILABLE FROM
THE EDITORS OF
POPULAR MECHANICS

This series celebrates vintage boy- and girlhood with a miscellany of marvelous ideas. From kites, toboggans, and backyard carnivals to science experiments, camping tips, and magic tricks, this collection of projects from *Popular Mechanics*' issues of long ago captures all the appeal of American ingenuity at the start of the last century.

$9.95 (CAN $10.95)
ISBN 978-1-58816-610-4

$9.95 (CAN $12.95)
ISBN 978-1-58816-509-1

$9.95 (CAN $10.95)
ISBN 978-1-58816-754-5

$9.95 (CAN $10.95)
ISBN 978-1-58816-703-3

$9.95 (CAN $10.95)
ISBN978-1-58816-639-5

$9.95 (CAN $12.95)
ISBN 978-1-58816-771-2

Library of Congress Cataloging-in-Publication Data
Popular mechanics how to charm a bird : create a backyard haven with
birdhouses, baths, and feeders / by the editors of Popular Mechanics.
      p. cm.
  Includes index.
  ISBN 978-1-58816-720-0
1. Bird attracting. 2. Bird watching. I. Popular mechanics (Chicago, Ill. :
1959) II. Title: How to charm a bird.
  QL676.5.P67 2009
  639.9'78--dc22

                                2009011564

10 9 8 7 6 5 4 3 2 1

Published by Hearst Books
A division of Sterling Publishing Co., Inc.
387 Park Avenue South, New York, NY 10016

Popular Mechanics is a registered trademark of Hearst Communications, Inc.

www.popularmechanics.com

For information about custom editions, special sales, premium and
corporate purchases, please contact Sterling Special Sales Department
at 800-805-5489 or specialsales@sterlingpublishing.com.

Distributed in Canada by Sterling Publishing
c/o Canadian Manda Group, 165 Dufferin Street
Toronto, Ontario, Canada M6K 3H6

Distributed in Australia by Capricorn Link (Australia) Pty. Ltd.
P.O. Box 704, Windsor, NSW 2756 Australia

Manufactured in China

Sterling ISBN 978-1-58816-720-0